Steam Days In Dorset

Above: Not in Dorset, but on its way! 'Merchant Navy' Class No. 35018 *British India Line* arrives at Southampton with 'The Bournemouth Belle'. This locomotive was the first to be rebuilt into a more conventional form. It is seen here in its as-built guise. *L. Elsey*
Below: Standard Class '4' tank No. 80134 waits in Bournemouth MPD yard.

ISBN 0 946184 96 8   Copyright Michael Webb & Waterfront   November 2002
Publisher Roger Hardingham
Printed by The Amadeus Press, Cleckheaton, West Yorkshire

Steam Days In Dorset

Michael Webb

With Photographs by

George Marsh

'M7' No. 30127 is seen at Bournemouth West, complete with Bournemouth shedcode. No. 30127 was one of fourteen 'M7s' allocated to Bournemouth in early 1963. She was withdrawn in November of that year.

Published by
Waterfront
A Division of Kingfisher Productions
The Dalesmade Centre, Watershed Mill, Settle, North Yorkshire BD24 9LR

CONTENTS

Dedication

I am more than blessed with people who have been willing to give up some of their precious time to help me in the preparation of my manuscript. My heartfelt thanks to them all, to my wife, Evelyn, for correcting many of my miss-spellings and placing the punctuations where they should have been; to my late sister-in-law, Margaret Speed, who then set about re-typing but was taken ill and sadly died before completion; to a good friend, Kathleen Rosier, who volunteered to take on and complete this task; to my daughter, Susan Chapman, who then committed it to a word processor; to another good friend, Lorna Foreman, for printing the completed disc.

    I am also very fortunate to have a friend, that doyen among railway photographers, George Marsh. When he learnt that I was writing a book, he told me that I was free to use any of his photographs from his collection. An offer to illustrate the book for me was an offer too good to turn down - thank you George. Finally, to my publisher Roger Hardingham, who has turned all of the components into the book in front of you now.

Introduction

To my readers may I propose the following toast: "To the past good friends, for I have experienced nothing like it at the present, nor do I contemplate doing so in the foreseeable future."

In my quieter moments I sometimes sit down with my memories and wonder if they ever happened at all. Almost everything connected with my first twenty five years working on the railway has now disappeared, not too many material things remain to prove that they ever existed. Politics decide what the policies of our railways will be, very inexperienced advisers concerned with curbing expenditure advising politicians, and yet it was once very different ......

You may have already gathered by now that I am by nature an old fashioned person and from an early age have not taken to change very gladly. Having said that, I have had to accept that with the knowledge and technology available to the modern railway engineers that changes would be made in the name of progress that would not always be to my way of thinking. Steam locomotives, for which the railways were built, would be replaced in an almighty hurry by the more modern forms of traction, namely diesel and electric.

It was my experience that the many types of machines constructed with the aid of that said knowledge and technology have been proved to be a great deal less reliable that what is required for the successful running of a modern railway system, causing delays, cancellations and general chaos to the timetables that would not have been accepted by the operating chiefs of yesteryear.

In conversation with passengers I was told many times that they would welcome back what is now termed 'The old steam days' and would gladly sacrifice time saved for the reliability and the near certainty that the train would run. Many of the older passengers mourned the loss of the dining cars on the trains and the cooked meals, especially breakfast, that could be obtained on them. Most are not placated by the arrival of the one-manned buffet cars or the trolleys with their plastic cups and plastic glasses, microwave assisted pies and burgers which have replaced the varied menus which were once available.

I know that I am biased but I will not condone what I term as the premature end of those 'steam days' which I am convinced were brought about by a then anti steam brigade, apostles of that so called saviour of railways (not my description) Dr Beeching. I think you will agree that history has proved that to save the taxpayers money then the wholesale destruction of the British railway system with the cuts and slashings, have proved a costly and total failure. Many parts of the country were left with no forms of transport system whatsoever, Dr Beeching failed to integrate road and rail services as was promised that would be of benefit to all the rural areas where the rail services had been withdrawn, achieving what any school child of very tender age could have achieved by going along lines that, if it didn't pay, then remove it.

His departure from the scene did not seem to alter things a lot, railways continued to run at a loss, the 'powers that be' decided on another line of approach to tackle the problem, not to close the stations but to take all the staff away from them and call them 'open stations' with only the bare necessities remaining e.g. a platform. Great changes are promised, sectorisation is now upon us and privatisation is just round the corner, where I wonder will it all end?

The author in front of Hamworthy signalbox.

Chapter One

Early Memories

I have often said when in conversation with my colleagues over the past few years that I could write a book on all that has happened to me in my railway career. I am not given to be a writer, nor am I any great scholar and have unlearnt many of the finer points of grammar that I was taught at school. Bearing this in mind, dear reader, I ask your forgiveness for the many grammatical errors that will confront you in the following pages. I only hope that I can convey to you in my own way a chronicle of the memories and experiences that have come my way during the fifty years and eight months of service on the railway. I have gained a wealth of experience along the way, taught by some of the most gifted men that anyone could wish to be associated with, I include in that statement the many ladies that were colleagues during the dark days of the war and the many that stayed on afterwards.

The urge to record down on paper what remains in my memory came recently when passing the site of the old Wimborne station, I could hardly credit that a thriving station that I once knew so well had ever existed. A station that once was the soul of this market town employing at one time over a hundred of its folk and provided services to many of its tradesmen. It is now all completely levelled and all traces removed from the face of the earth. Sacrilege followed in its wake when after the demolition, a small industrial estate was built at one end and a housing estate at the other. I have said that all traces had been removed, not so, as I was to find out a few weeks later.

A short walk has been laid out from Station Road to the rivers edge and a part of the old Poole sidings remains at the same level as once the rest of the area was, where one may see just how far they had to go to getto the level of the road. I was pleasantly surprised on climbing up the bank to see among the trees and shrubs that had sprung up since the closure of the line, a short points line with the bases, and a few rusty rods still in place.

Following along this line I discovered some signal wires still in the pulleys, sentimentally I thought, waiting to be reconnected to some imaginary signal and longing to be at work again. Silly old soft me, but they were the same rods and wires that were connected to the levers in the signal box that I used to operate all those years ago, firstly as a young nipper under the watchful eye of the signalman and then as relief signalman in my own right some fourteen years later. Enough of all this sentimentality and on to the job in hand.

My arrival at Wimborne station on the morning of Thursday November 19th 1942 was the culmination of a passion that had been within me since early childhood. I had been fascinated by the sight and the sound of the trains at the bottom of our garden when we lived in Langley Road at Branksome, and then in a lane next to the Woodman Hotel just off of Poole Road, the main line from Bournemouth West being only a few yards away at the end of that lane. Branksome station was only a few yards away from our house as well and it was there from the footbridge that crossed the lines that Noel, my next door neighbour and I first took up the serious business of watching trains. We never did scribble down numbers, satisfaction was obtained from just seeing the trains come and go. I can remember to this day the names of the two porters on duty in those days, they were Harry Burt and Ted Marsh.

No objections were ever raised to our presence but when we were convinced that eyes were not observing, and boys being boys, we would 'sneak' down on to one of the platforms to get a little closer, quite illegal of course in the absence of a penny platform ticket required under the bye laws for such an excursion. This requirement was well beyond our very limited income, the only money that ever came my way was a penny on a Friday when my father came home from the dole office, he being one of the many thousands that could not find work in those troubled days. We were of course seen not to be in our usual place and a voice would call from the top of the stairs to 'get back up here or else'. Admonished for our trespass but gladly not banished for our sins we would sheepishly wander away for a while, later returning hoping that our misdoings had been forgotten as they always were.

Drummond Class 'M7' No. 30112 is station pilot at Bournemouth Central during 1960.

My lasting memories of the station are of many brightly coloured posters adorning the platforms proclaiming the delights of travelling by trains and informing all their readers that 'There is more room remember in June and September', many would conclude with the words 'Our aim is your satisfaction'. I suppose that even in those pre-war days it was to your advantage to stagger your holidays and to be sure of a seat instead of perhaps having to stand for most of the journey. Things have not changed all that much have they?

Handbills in the Booking Hall advertised the times and prices to many local destinations and quite a few farther afield to where excursions prices were said to be 'second to none'. These handbills became collectors items and were eagerly snapped up as each new one appeared on the hook, this only occurring when it was certain that the coast was clear. Always a temptation to young lads hands was a bell push built into the wall close to the Booking Hall door with a highly polished brass and wooden surround inscribed with the words 'Press button to call porters'. It could have been a target for mischievous hands had there been a convenient place to hide after such a prank, but there was not, and so our luck was not pushed that far and neither was the bell.

Painful memories recall that I once received a cuff alongside the earhole by the local bobby for running across the road bridge over the railway in front of a car, and told that the next time would lead me to the Court. I remember the incident sometimes, I never did repeat it, so it must have done me some good, though I wonder what would happen if it took place today, angry parents of the 'victim' would be suing the policeman for assault most likely, I'm certainly glad now that it happened to me for it certainly taught me a lesson.

One other such happening when Noel and I were exposing ourselves to the dangers of the road was to be the beginning of one of the most happy and contented periods of my life. We had stepped off the pavement in Bourne Valley Road to get a better view of a train passing over the bridge when we were befriended by a tall grey haired lady, somewhat concerned for the safety of two young lads, and suggested that we could watch the trains from a much safer place than the road. We had no idea of where she lived but any apprehensions that we may have had were soon dispelled as she led us under the bridge, through a gate close by and up a long garden path to a small cottage that had been built slap bang in the middle of what would be known in railway jargon as the Branksome triangle and within a very few feet of the railway lines.

This vantage point proved to be beyond our wildest dreams. In many months that followed many blissful hours were spent on a pile of sleepers next to the fence watching trains. A goods siding leading from Branksome yard to the main line was close by and it would have been possible to touch the engines as they went up and down with their shunting duties. It was not long before we became known to some of those Engine crews and a word from a driver or fireman caused much satisfaction and a warm feeling inside that such 'Gods' had spoken to us.

The signal box was but a few yards away opposite, as was a siding leading to Sharp Jones Pottery, which was sometimes shunted twice a day, quite a bonus for an appreciative audience. Being in the middle of the Branksome triangle meant that we had a view of signals for trains to and from Bournemouth West and Bournemouth Central and we only had to look directly behind us to see trains crossing the other viaduct between Gas Works junction and Bournemouth West junction, first to hear the loud exhaust as they laboured up the bank from Bournemouth and then to see the black smoke from the chimneys as the regulators were eased to negotiate the sharp curve across the junction, a sight indeed. It was an education to read some of the names on the sides of the goods wagons as they went by, I can remember some of those names to this day and some that I had forgotten, I am reminded of by some of the model railways on display today.

My lovely lady benefactor who enabled us to enjoy those childhood days was a Mrs Hawes who was the wife of a Guard stationed at Bournemouth West who was to become a very valued colleague in later years, as was their son who served his time in the clerical grade in the many stations where I was privileged to be at the same time. My appreciation for her kindness and for her concern for the safety of two young boys have not diminished with the passing of the years, although she has long since rightly attained her place among the angels. I never did know if it was that we should return after that first morning but the next day and for many a long day afterwards a knock on the door and a request that 'please could we watch the trains' was never refused.

The loco-shed at Branksome with the signalbox at Bournemouth West Junction on the far right.

Above: An early photograph of Bournemouth West station which was closed in 1965. This 19th century view shows the 1874-built station in all its splendour. The only recognisable building still standing today, is the one of the left which is now Queens Hall. The Midland Hotel is behind the camera.

Below: A London & South Western scene in all its glory. Here an Adams 4-4-0, with a set of non corridor carriages, approaches Meyrick Park Halt.

Chapter Two
As It Was In The Beginning

As with all things the halcyon summer days of childhood came to an end far too soon, brought abruptly to an end by the advent of World War Two. The family had also moved away from the railway to a place in Alder Road, not so far away that I could not hear the trains as they crossed the viaducts at Bourne Valley Road or on a quiet night ascending Parkstone bank. It may come as some surprise to you that my first job on leaving school in July 1942 was in a small farm building a few yards away from home that had been commandeered by the War Department for the manufacture of shell bases used in the big guns on board Royal Navy ships. This was ideal for me in the circumstances, not too far away from home, no travelling expenses, and a weekly pay of some twenty five shillings. The work force consisted of the Manager, Mr Bailey, his daughter, two young ladies who lived just up the road from me, and three men.

I was never very sure what my job exactly was, I was firstly employed at keeping the surrounds of the machine clear of metal filings, impossible to do while they were being operated, make tea a couple of times a day and generally making myself useful in anything that might crop up. Just watching for a lot of the time was very boring for a young lad of my age but it was obvious that if I became too knowledgeable I could do someone out of a job and having got one of those nice little wartime jobs it became essential that they kept it, so it was in everybody's interest that I was not educated further into the arts of machinery. A few weeks of trying to look busy culminated in Mr Bailey deciding that perhaps after all I was surplus to his requirement, and it was better that I leave. I wasn't sorry really but I must admit that the stigma of getting the sack at such an early stage of my life did not go down too well, but I did turn down the chance to go back after my mother had been to see Mr Bailey and explained that I could have been capable of better things had I been taught the right way.

It was my father who one day suggested that I write to his old Stationmaster at Bournemouth West and ask if there were any openings for a 14 year old boy on the railway. A welcome letter arrived a week or so later with the good news that a vacancy existed at Wimborne for the position of a number taker, and, subject to attending the Company's doctor at Southampton and satisfying him, then the job could be mine.

Urie Class 'H15' No. 30476 sits on shed at Bournemouth in 1960 No. 30476 was built in 1924 and was one of the last four 'H15s' in service, being withdrawn in December 1961.

Above: A view of the Motive Power Depot at Bournemouth from within in shed area. A number of locomotives are 'on shed' and as usual the running lines are busy with traffic.

Below: 'West Country' Class No. 34042 *Dorchester* brings a train up from the west past the depot. The shed was labelled 71B until the end of its life in 1967. A dual carriageway, Wessex Way, now passes over the site.

Fresh in my mind to this day I well remember catching the 8.10 a.m. to be greeted on the platform by the Stationmaster, Mr Carter. My first words, 'Good, morning sir ,I've come to work' seemed to amuse him somewhat and he bade me follow him down some steps, through a subway, up some more steps and along the opposite platform,across a couple of lines into a small grey bricked building known as the goods office and which was to be my headquarters for the next few months. Once inside I warmed to a nice fire in the grate at the far end of the room and was introduced to the occupants.

Sitting on a high stool to the right of the room was a Mr Johnson who I was informed was the Chief Goods Clerk and forever afterwards I would address as 'Mr J.'. The next person I was introduced to was a Frank Bailey who was the checker in the warehouse or goods shed as it was known, next to be made known to me

Breakdown train vehicles stationed at Bournemouth MPD.

was a Jack Ingram who was a checker in the goods yard, and finally the man who I was about to replace, Bob Penny, who if my memory serves me right was leaving to join one of the Services, I think it was the Royal Navy. Mr J. was to be my immediate superior and a very good boss he turned out to be, a very busy man, he was responsible for all the traffic that passed through the yard and warehouse and often had to work long after normal hours to keep it all up to date.

My training was brief before I had to take over on my own and not really as it should have been. I don't think that in all fairness Bob was too well educated in the procedure and was only passing on what he had been taught about it, but as in my time at the factory, proved to be very unsatisfactory. Number taking does not sound much of an important job does it?, but it really was in those days. The contents on a form that was made out by the number taker, after going round the yard and all the sidings, had to be phoned through to a central office in the divisional buildings at Southampton before mid-day to be analysed.

Information on this form informed them of the number of wagons on hand on that particular day, wagons that had arrived since the day before, wagons that had been sent away since rendering the last return as the form was known, the different types of wagons, whether they were loaded or empty, and if empty were they required to be re-loaded with some other commodity or were they surplus to that stations' requirements. If so they would become available to be sent somewhere else and orders could be

given for their dispatch.

One column on the return was the 'U' column, this involved anticipating, based on the previous days figures, the number of wagons that might become empty and perhaps be required for re-loading or become spare and available for where that particular type of wagon maybe required. It was nearly impossible to keep everything up square as the saying is. Goods trains came and went after I had gone home at 5.00 p.m., the yard had been shunted a couple of times before my arrival at 8.40 a.m. and many things had happened beyond my control. It was not unusual for a tarpaulin sheet or a rope to be thrown back into an empty wagon and sent away as 'empty'. Those items were also included on the daily wagon return, and, being railway property, were also charged for and debited to the receiving station.

Pieces of wood used to scotch anything that might

The familiar tight curve at Poole station in the 1960s with a BR Standard Class '5', No. 73029, about to head east.

move in transit were debited and had to be returned to the forwarding station, some not much better than firewood, some not so good but they all had to be paid for, so you can imagine the rigmarole that went on when they were sent away in an empty wagon by a careless shunter or come who may. The labels on one side of the wagon were always taken off by the yard checker on the day of arrival and details entered into a book that was kept by him, this being his proof of arrival, and then passed to Mr J. to check against an Invoice from the forwarding station, and entered into a station book for the consignee to sign for, received in good order or not. In the absence of labels on this one side it was not unknown for a loaded wagon to be sent away as empty and then you may guess the sparks that would fly. Some poor chap would come in next morning to finish off unloading his wagon and there it was, gone.

Part of my territory included the military sidings at Merley which was the site of the old Somerset and Dorset railways locomotive depot and now in use by the War Department, staffed by troops of the 52nd Pioneer Corps. I can recall the Sergeant in charge of one platoon who were working in the sidings, he was always referred to as 'ginger'. I had some idea that he was a cockney by birth and as with most kids of my age at the time I was prone to taking the 'mickey' a little bit because his three stripes and was lucky sometimes not to get a belt around the ears for my cheeky remarks. It must have been that he had attained a good sense of humour, because I never did.

These sidings were served daily by the 8.30 a.m. goods from Poole and the 2.00 p.m. goods from Hamworthy Junction, and it was this train that nearly spelt my early demise one afternoon. I was walking across the river bridge on my way up to check the wagons not taking a lot of notice as to where I was walking, when I suddenly looked up and saw the goods train a few feet away, my deliverance was secured by a good turn of speed back towards the station, and taking refuge in the short siding at the end of the bridge.

I watched the train go by and realised that the crew had not seen me from first to last, hence no whistle of warning. I can still remember the engine number, it was No. 612, an Adams 'Jubilee' class, I was to come across it many times after that, only in much safer circumstances.

There had to be a fly in the ointment, as the saying is, in every occupation, and mine came in the shape of a wagon inspector, by the name of Jock Habgood. Jock had attained this position due to losing an arm in an accident at Wareham whilst he was a Guard. In later years he was to become a very god friend and mentor to me, but in those days, as I have mentioned before, my education into the intricacies of making out this wagon return was not as it should have been and it was the job of Jock to visit each station in turn to make sure that what was in the yard was on the return as rendered, and it was only too often that when he came to Wimborne things didn't tally at all, which meant that on observing his arrival the signal to beat a hasty retreat until you hoped that he had gone was given. Not always successful, he would appear at the most inopportune time, no chance of escape and then the music had to be faced.

Friday afternoon meant that the weekly demurrage return had to be compiled, signed by Mr J., and then sent away to Divisional Offices at Southampton. This return recorded all the wagons that had taken over the 48 hours allowed for unloading. In agreement with Mr J., I would quite often leave off wagons from this return belonging to old Mr Farwell and Mr Blaney, two local Coal Merchants, all done in secret you will understand. Old Mr Farwell only had a horse and cart to load his sacks of coal on before trading them around the town, and both horse and master were showing signs of old age, as was the ancient old Morris Commercial that Mr Blaney had as transport and capable of carrying only a few sacks at a time.

The consignee's of all the wagons entered on this return would be sent a bill for detaining the wagon(s) longer than the

An atmospheric shot as No. 73029 departs from Poole across the level crossing which cuts Towngate Street in half.

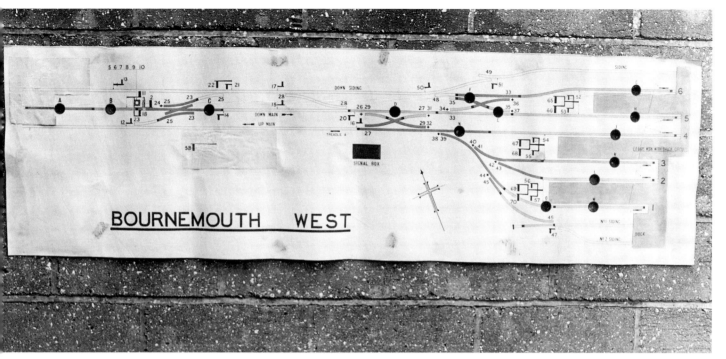

The signalling diagram of Bournemouth West Station showing the layout including the lines to the six platforms.

48 hours allowed, and so to temper justice with a little mercy it became my practice not to enter a wagon into the daily arrivals book until sometimes a couple of days after I should have done, or perhaps Mr J., would say 'leave it off the form this week, it might be empty by Monday' and then of course it was not unusual for Jock to arrive and find a half emptied wagon that had been booked out as empty. It was not unusual to get orders to send a wagon or some tarpaulin sheets to somewhere or other and then to discover that it, or they, were not available because they were not ready or already had gone somewhere else, possibly by mistake or possibly by having to arrange the figures so that they agreed with the other columns on the daily stock return.

There were exceptions to this, quite often a wagon would arrive of a particular type that was in very short supply and high demand, particularly those that could convey military traffic such as Bren gun carriers or lorries or cars, and then we would receive orders for their dispatch before arrival and then it was my job to make sure that the appropriate labels were made out and the wagon labelled as soon as it was cleared, and woe betide anybody causing any hiccup to this instruction. All wagons that could carry coal were sent to a 'Pool', L.M.S. Pool and routed via Bath, work welcomed by the old Somerset and Dorset railway.

Two young ladies, of whom I have so far made no mention, assisted Frank Bailey in the warehouse, Margaret Shakesby and Gladys Bartlett, Margaret came to Wimborne from Gainsborough in Lincolnshire and lived in the town with a married sister. She was later to become one of the first lady guards at Bournemouth and marry one of our young firemen there, Cliff Bailey. Gladys Bartlett was the wife of a permanent way platelayer at Wimborne and lived in the Station house. Two lorry drivers, George Northover and

Leslie Goodall completed the complement. George lived locally in Station Road and Leslie commuted each day from Ringwood.

The two young ladies were more than capable of handling the heavy loads that they had to deal with every day, and when it came to pitting my strength against theirs it was no match. It befell my lot at times to assist them to unload wagons of cattle food consigned to either Silcocks or Thorleys who had premises on either side of the warehouse or to help position barrels of tar that occasionally arrived to the order of a firm at Chard and through the goods office would be able to sell same to whoever required tar in those days.

These barrels weighed quite a lot, over a hundredweight, and had to be placed on a raised wooden platform on the station side of the warehouse. It was embarrassing at times to see the ease in which they went about things, and I was loath to admit it but they had no competition from me again when the tar barrels had to be moved. We saw a lot of Frank Bailey in the goods office, all goods received and forwarded were invoiced and part of his job was to see that everything that was invoiced arrived in good condition and to advise forwarding stations that the invoice had arrived, but not the goods, and as you may guess that happened frequently in those war time days. Much of the correspondence was passed through a small window in the passage way of the office if it was inconvenient for Frank to make his way into the office and sometimes a message for him would be dealt with in this way, a sort of a jungle telegraph system as we christened it ....

Jack Ingram proved to be a good tutor as far as I was concerned, he taught me how to take the tarpaulin sheet from a wagon and then to fold it in a certain fashion so as to place it on top of any load, and it would open up and drop over the sides ready to be tied down. When these sheets became wet they were very heavy and one had to be a mini Atlas to get them on top of the wagons, there was also a special way for ropes to be tied to any large loads that were being forwarded, sometimes several ropes had to be used on one item and it was a work of art making sure that nothing would move in the many shunting movements that took place along the journey.

Another thing I was taught by Jack was how to operate the small hand crane that was in the yard, there was also two more in the warehouse, and it would not have been the first

their next load whenever they came into the yard from anywhere. By the time I was sixteen years old I was quite proficient at it.

Before I came to Wimborne I always imagined it to be a sleepy little town that only came to life on a Tuesday, market day. I probably had the same opinion of the station as well, but the next few months was to rudely shatter that illusion. It was a base for many of the local Traders and for many of the Contractors engaged in the building of the airfield at Tarrant Rushton, the military hospitals at Kingston Lacey and St. Leonards, the London Brick Company transported the bricks to the hospital sites, Wimpeys all the materials required at

The once busy junction at Templecombe. Racing from right to left is a Bulleid un-rebuilt Pacific on the main Salisbury to Exeter route. In the foreground is the depot at Templecombe with four of the S&DJR '7F' 2-8-0s present. A Southern 'G6' tank is on the far left.

time that someone had been hurt when the handle flew off, or the person operating the brake let the load down too fast or in the wrong place, it was always the rule that only competent persons were allowed to operate the cranes, but when needs must this rule was not always adhered to, occasionally with the result that someone did get hurt. One more concession that I enjoyed was driving the two lorries up and down the yard. One was a three ton Bedford that Les Goodall drove and the other was a three wheeled Scammel 'mechanical horse' as they were known, driven locally by George Northover. I used to badger these two men to let me turn them round in the yard and place them in position for

Tarrant Rushton, the latter firm employing many Irishmen.

Besides the two Coal Merchants that I have already mentioned, E.T. Evans and Mackays Glasshouse Properties also unloaded coal, Stanley Pond the agricultural engineers, situated in the Station Terrace, often received farm implements and machinery by rail as did Dorset Farmers, who had a depot at the end of No. 3 road, almost opposite to the warehouse. Wagons for this firm would be placed when possible on the stopblock of this road to facilitate easier unloading.

The Forestry Commission also loaded away pitprops to the coal mines in Northern England, Scotland and Wales. The two firms dealing in sacks of cattle feed, Silcocks and Thorleys, they seemed to have depots in all the railway yards in Southern and SouthWest England, were always busy, individual farmers would collect, or our railway lorry would have to be loaded, for delivery to some outlying farm in the area.

I remember that on one Sunday I was booked on to help Les Goodall to take a couple of loads out to a farm at Almer, a welcome few shillings overtime for a nipper in those days, in addition to the fourteen shillings and three pence which was my basic pay. I was not too happy when handling these particular products as some of the sacks went at a hundredweight and a half, too heavy for me to stack one upon the other, but it had to be done. You may guess that I was only too glad to get some help from the two ladies at times, but never did like showing that I couldn't manage it when they showed it was only childs play to them. Yes, it was very much a hive of industry for what it was, a small country station, which had played no small part in the country's war effort, and in its own way still had a part to play before the war ended.

It was now late in 1943, and plans were then afoot for the launching of 'D' day, although we didn't know it. Experienced railway men would be required in the shunting yards of the intended ports of embarkation, and so it was that it was not long before our own Jack Ingram and Ernie Livermore from the Parcels Office would be leaving us to help in the great movement of fighting men and machines from our shores. The man replacing Jack on the yard was Fred Wayman, who came to us via the wartime Essential Works Act, his previous occupation being a chauffeur to one of the landed gentry, replacing Ernie in the Parcels Office was a very attractive young lady, the wife of a serving soldier, Beryl Bradley.

Fred fitted in very well with the job and proved to be a very capable and very popular member of the staff with a gifted sense of humour. He and I became great pals and I sorely missed him when my turn came to leave Wimborne. The presence of Beryl Bradley in the Parcel Office caused quite a stir among many of the young bucks in the locality, here for the first time ever was a lady porter and a pretty one at that. I will add that she impressed me as well, but all credit to her loyalty to her soldier husband, she stood no nonsense from any of us, but nevertheless she had quite a lot of help when it came to lifting anything heavy and pushing loaded barrows up the slope to the platforms.

If my memory serves me correctly, Beryl only worked for a set number of hours and not as long as Ernie Livermore did, and so it was decided that I would be transferred to the Parcel Office, and another lad taken on to do my job. Tuition by Beryl was a pleasure as you might have guessed, only too short though, and then I took over on the opposite shift, the start of my dealing with the general public at large and what a baptism it turned out to be.

The telephone on my desk proved to be a problem that I could have done without, the train enquiries that I had to

'West Country' Class No. 34006 *Bude* brings its train over the iron bridge at Wimborne, with the River Stour passing beneath.

The interesting layout at Broadstone station is seen in this photograph looking north. The 'South Western signals were a pleasant feature at Broadstone for many years. A BR Standard locomotive brings in a train from the Wimborne direction. The single line disappearing to the left is the route towards Corfe Mullen and Blandford. The line in the left foreground is to Hamworthy Jct. *Ron Lumber*

answer I quite often had to seek help from a busy Booking Clerk for I had not yet mastered the mysteries of many timetables, and I must confess now that I don't think I ever did. However, some of my colleagues in that office were very co-operative and some not so, 'oh tell them to change at Brockenhurst, arriving at London at sometime or other and ask when they get there' would be their reply. Well you can only pass on what you were told, which I did, and I don't recall any complaint from irate passengers of not arriving at where they were supposed to go.

The two clerks in the Booking Office were Albert Jeffries and a Mr Smith, his forename I cannot recall, he had an artificial leg, I remember, but did not stay in the Booking Office very long before he transferred to Oakley crossing as a crossing keeper. Albert, who lived at Broadstone, had two sons who were later to become railway men, Terry had to retire early after becoming a guard at Bournemouth, ill health I believe, and Gordon left the railway after a short time to become a policeman. He too retired from that force due to ill health and died at quite an early age. Albert went on to become Stationmaster firstly at Moreton and then

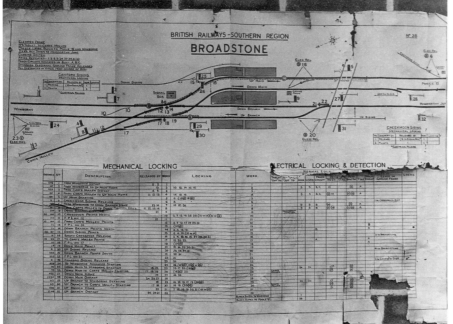

The signalling diagram from 1954 at Broadstone showing the routes north and south.

Above: Verwood station on the Salisbury-Fordingbridge-Wimborne route. This was typical of a later style LSWR country station. Note the signalbox 'wedged' in between the station building and the wooden goods shed. The line on the right is the passing loop.
Below: An early view of Ringwood station with its well-known footbridge dominating the scene. The starting signal on the far right is the Christchurch line. The photographer is standing by New Street crossing.

'West Country' Class No. 34006 *Bude* hauls a special train past Ringwood signalbox. The train crosses over Christchurch Road.

at Hamworthy Goods. On his retirement that depot came under the supervision of the Stationmaster at Poole.

The vacancy at Wimborne was taken by a young man from the London area, Charlie Layton, he had a great sense of humour which seemed to rub off on everyone that he worked with, he was also destined to marry the Stationmaster's daughter. The position on the opposite shift took a long time to fill, and seemed to be covered by relief men, mainly Harold Silverthorne from New Milton and Ronald Young from Christchurch, both very helpful to me in my early days in the Parcel Office and in my absence attending trains, they would accept parcels from customers, and when I came back they were all ready to go, stamped and booked in.

I remember one night I played a prank on Ron; he had taken a young lady, who shall remain nameless, for a walk as the homeward train was running late, I decided that I would call out that the train had left the 'Moors' (West Moors) which caused him to cut short his walk and run back to the station. Of course when he arrived and looked at the signal, still red, he enquired of Sam in the signal box as to the precise location of my presence, little knowing that I was hidden in the depths of the box listening to all that he was saying, if his knowledge of the box had been good at that time he could have just opened the door a foot or so away and all would have been revealed, and the culprit 'copped'. I was thankful that Ron had a good sense of humour for I had to go on the

same train home some time later. In later years I was to meet up with them both in various places but eventually lost touch when returning to Wimborne in 1955, which was a pity, I valued their friendship very much, two very likeable men.

I had to be indoctrinated into the railway book-keeping system, where to enter cash received, how to make out accounts, how to issue left luggage tickets, and left bicycles, and then to balance the books at the end of each shift and make sure the monies in the till was the same as the cash total in the book, I don't think that I was out very often. As with the goods side, the passenger department also had their

regular customers, a young apprentice, Len Applin, who I still have the pleasure of meeting, would come to the office frequently with cases of heavy machinery from J. Flowers, which had to be lifted from his sack truck on to the scales to be weighed before being stamped with the appropriate amount of stamps pasted on and then pushed up the slope to the platform to await a train.

Every now and again one would have to go on a down train and then it befell my lot to lift it across the lines on to the opposite platform. When Len had time he would give a shove up the slope to ease my burden but he didn't always have time. Cartons of clothes from a firm in the town, Johnsons, were sent away two or three times a week to their depot at Liverpool for cleaning, which in due course we would get back. Mrs Young who kept a fish and chip shop in the town, also worked for the Bursar at Canford School, would meet the 1.22 p.m. from Bournemouth West which would arrive about 1.55 p.m. and collect a churn of milk for the school. This churn would, whenever possible, be loaded onto a dreadnought, a four-wheeled flat truck, so that it was easier to unload into the old Morris Commercial van. They were heavy objects when they were full, and I always tried to be there when the train arrived, but I think that Mrs Young handled it better when I wasn't there than when I was. She was a very nice lady and once again was the wife of a serving serviceman, the Royal Air Force, if memory serves me rightly.

A local colourful character by the name of Mr Shepard was also one of our regulars on a Tuesday, he was a well built man, suffering from some sort of asthmatic complaint, he seemed to know everyone and everyone knew him. His arrival in the office with the calves that he had purchased at the market signalled the need for a small inhaler that he kept in his pocket to be used, a few puffs of that and then business commenced.

The calves would arrive with a small split sack tied round their middle and after finding out the cost of transit stamps would be attached to a label tied round its neck and then coaxed but mainly pulled, up the slope to await the train. Assistance always had to be sought to load the animals into the guards van, one on either side with one hand under its neck, the other under its middle, and into the van, this procedure had to be repeated at Brockenhurst and many other places en route as quite a number of calves were destined to a place in Sussex, I don't think that Wimborne was a very popular place for many of the guards on a Tuesday; the van had to be washed out before leaving Brockenhurst on the return journey.

A Mr Kemp who lived in the Avenue, and was a local reporter for the Western Gazette came in regularly with a small envelope addressed to his paper at Yeovil, there was a special rate for this which came under the newspaper scale and used to cost him somewhere about just over a shilling.

Two local fishmongers in the town, Claude Brown and Mac Fisheries were also good customers, but due to the blitz on the cities in those days the fish didn't always arrive, and when it did it was sometimes in the evening, too late to sell, and then the 'No fish' signs would be in the windows together with the 'No beer, No cigarettes' signs only too familiar in the early 1940's. I can remember the newspapers not arriving until nearly tea time on some days. Mrs Young

also depended on the railway for supplies of fish, and often it would be pea fritters and chips only when she opened up her shop.

Cartons of Lyons cakes would arrive for the N.A.A.F.I. stores in the Army camp at Merley, British and American troops were stationed in that area, it was occasionally my luck to accompany George Northover in delivering these cartons and as he had got to know the ladies in charge up there we would be rewarded with a cup of tea and a bun when there was one going. A further duty that I was entrusted with was on a Friday when I was on the later turn, I would have to go across to Mr Whiffen's and get George Rolls, one of the signalmen in the signal box, and ounce of 'Digger' tobacco and the Western Gazette, it came to about eleven pence I think.

There seemed to be a steady flow of passengers using the station in those days, weekends would see many of the troops going home on leave, or many of the American troops making their way up to London to see the sights, or so they used to say, even in the war we had commuters and school children travelling to Poole or Bournemouth in the morning, returning in the evening and there was not many trains that someone did not join or get off throughout the day.

The staff on the traffic (passenger) side of the station were made up of two lady porteresses, Mary and Grace Brown, no relation, George Rolls and Sam Upward, the two signalmen, Ralph Allen who was classed as a Porter signalman among many other things, George White, porter come lampman come assistant shunter, and the head shunter Wesley Evans. Mary Brown was once again the wife of a serving soldier, a pretty dark haired girl of some late twenties I would have said, although I am not really very good at guessing ladies ages. If I did have a favourite in those times then Mary was that, she gave the impression that she was more than a little concerned for the safety of her man away in the war and the absence of a letter from him was the cause of much apprehension and anxiety. I recall that one afternoon while helping to unload one of Mrs Youngs milks churns it slipped off of the barrow and the milk was spilt all over the platform, poor Mary burst into tears and was inconsolable for most of that afternoon.

Her opposite number, Grace Brown, was as different as chalk from cheese as the saying is, a small bubbly sort of girl and about the same age as Mary, she knew nearly everyone that came to the station and nearly everyone knew Grace, very popular with the train crews and stood no nonsense from anyone. I learnt a lot of railway work from these two young ladies and was able to carry out many of my duties the better for it.

The two men I was to know as 'Chuckle' White and 'Knacker' Allen, I never did get to know how they came to be so christened. George White was not far off retiring age when I came there but he was just as sprite and nimble as a man half his age, he used to climb up the signal posts to change the lamps in all weathers. He was a tall, well built man, he looked strong even though he was getting on a bit, a very round face with a small moustache. To my mind he looked what a retired Army Colonel might look like, and so it was that I named him 'Colonel'.

I think that this proved to be very amusing on George's

part, and forever after when coming across him I would address him as such, and he would make a mock attempt to catch me saying 'I'll give you Colonel my sonny'. The trouble was that it was catching on with the older members of the staff to honour him with this rank, and whilst he didn't mind me doing it he didn't take too kindly to them. Whenever the gentry of the district travelled by train it always seemed that it was George that was on hand to carry their luggage to and from the cars, and I suspected well rewarded for his labours.

I sometimes wish that I had taken more notice of what he used to tell me of the old days, of when he was a boy and he had to fill up stoneware bottles to keep the passengers' feet warm in the winter, or climb along the tops of the carriages lighting the lamps and dropping them back inside. Primitive ways in those primitive days, but it is all history that has gone with the demise of those old railwaymen who were truly historians in their own right, yes, how I wish that I could remember what George related to me in some quieter moments.

My other colleague, Ralph Allen, was a much younger man, not in the Army I would have guessed, by being in a reserved occupation as the railways were in the war. It probably was as well, for Ralph was a jack of all trades at Wimborne and master of them all. He had passed out (certified as competent by an Inspector) for porter, lampman, shunter, guard and lorry driver. He was tall, slim built with dark wavy hair and a pencil moustache, and fairly popular with the ladies.

There is one particular incident concerning Ralph that sticks in my mind; recently arrived in the yard was an old lorry circa 1930's, from the Brighton area, and was to be used for relief purposes whenever the other vehicles were taken out of service for any reason. It must have been a five tonner, high off the road and built when they built them. However, being a relief driver, as they were known then, not a lorry driver but a motor driver, this lorry was a source of challenge to Ralph and one morning he decided that it was time that it was tried out. 'Coming for a ride nipper?' he said to me, 'I want to call round home and get some sandwiches that I left behind this morning'. Too good an opportunity to miss, I managed to scive off for a few minutes or so I thought that it may have been.

Unfortunately the old lorry proved to be more of a master for Ralph than he could manage, and turning left from Leigh Road into St Catherines proved to be his undoing, he went straight into Mr Banfield's iron fence on the corner and all but demolished it. A report of the accident would have to be made out, and it was put down to the steering being very stiff as he turned into Rodways garage to get some petrol, this, of course, would involve turning right, it didn't do much damage to the old lorry, bit of a bent mudguard which was soon hammered out; as I have said before, they built 'em in those days.

I was on tenterhooks for a while after this wondering if I would be in any trouble for being party to this misdemeanour but I never did get called to task over it. One of the sad things of life was that Ralph left the railway after the war, he was married by then and was killed in an accident on a building site in Bournemouth while driving a J.C.B. Great pity, for he was a darn good railwayman and I

felt that he would have gone much further up the scale than he did had he stayed on.

The two resident signalmen were of advanced age, George Rolls being the elder, and Sam Upward. George, who rode a bicycle from Broadstone each day, was fairly tall, well built and a very quiet and inoffensive sort of man, it always amazed me that at his time of life he chose to leave Wimborne for a guard's job at Bournemouth.

Sammy Upward was just the opposite, small, wiry and full of life, he used to let me have a pull of the levers whenever I went up aloft. I remember that once some wag sent me up to him to get some red and green oil for the signal lamps, he sent me back saying they were far too heavy for a lad to manage and that they'd better come up and get it themselves. I remember Sam for two things, one was that he also rode an old bicycle into work each day from Stapehill, and one day he decided that his trusty steed was now time expired and he had to have another one. The replacement machine was so much lighter than his old one and did not need as much pedalling to get it along, Sam regretted that for all those years he had worked like a demon as he put it to get it to go when all the time there was a machine available like this new one, 'wish I'd changed it before' he often lamented.

The second thing I remember him for was his love of a couple of slices of toast with a hunk of cheese in between and warmed up in the range oven, he would offer me some, but I couldn't stand the smell of it let alone eat it. I reasoned that Sam being still a bachelor would eat anything, what with that smell and an old pipe that he used to smoke, you can imagine how the old signal box could smell at times. Two shunters, one on the opposite shift to the other made up the staff complement of the station. I have already mentioned Wesley Evans, his opposite mate being Ted Woodford, both were later to leave Wimborne to become guards, Wesley at Bournemouth and Ted at Salisbury from where I believe he originated.

Before I left, two ladies were to join us, Doris Kimber and Marion Feltham. Doris was the wife of a serving soldier and had a young daughter who travelled by the train each day to and from Parkstone Grammar School, a very nice looking young lady, suffice to say that Doris was mum though. Marion Feltham was younger than Doris, remembering my previous remarks about ladies ages I'd say she was about nineteen and again a very nice looking lass she was. I think that Marion had to withstand a lot of unwanted attention from us young bucks of those days but she managed very well and I cannot recall any 'hanky panky' though it could not have been from the want of trying. Both of these ladies soon were very competent at their job, and I had good reason to be grateful to them both when they would lock up the Parcel Office last thing at night after putting away the parcels that came off of the last train, and by their doing just that I could go home on it.

I was once told that the stationmaster at Wimborne had one hundred and twelve staff on the payrolls at one time, he was also responsible for the crossing keepers at Canford, Uddens, Hayes Lane and Oakley. Attached to Wimborne station though not under the direct authority of the Stationmaster, were the Permanent Way Department, the Signal and Telegraph Department and the Carriage and

Wagon Department.

Each Department had a small wooden workshop which stood alongside Poole siding on the Broadstone side of the station. There was a small office on the down platform where Bert Haines, always known as 'Ginger' Haines, and his office lad, Jimmy Howell, held fort for the Permanent Way Department. It was my job to take any correspondence arriving on the trains for Inspector Haines to his office, and everything that arrived after his office had closed at 5.00 p.m. was placed in a pigeon hole in the Parcel Office as was all other things destined for the Signal and Telegraph Department and the Carriage and Wagon Department.

Employed at Wimborne on the Permanent Way as it was known, was their Inspector, Bert Haines, the ganger, Jim Emmet, sub ganger, Percy Brackstone, and platelayers Nan Stroud, Sam Barrow and Albert Hoare. Jim lived in one of the old Somerset and Dorset cottages close to Oakley Crossing, Percy was a sergeant on the local Home Guard unit in which most of his colleagues were attached, Nan Stroud later became a ganger on the next length up the line, in charge between Wimborne and West Moors. He was still there when I returned to Wimborne in 1955 and I came across him often when I relieved at Uddens.

I always thought that Nan was a darn good ganger and was pleased for him one day when he was asked to line up a curve in the old fashioned way with his eye along the rail after a series of complaints from drivers about the rough riding along that particular stretch of line. It was after a special type of board had been issued to each gang to assist them to align the cant on the curves. Nan didn't go a bundle on these new fangledthings as he called them, and told his Inspector in no uncertain terms that the best place for them

would be on the bonfire, but it was insisted that they be used so used they were, with the result that it was back to the old trusty eye before very much longer.

It wasn't long before Sam Barrow left Wimborne too, he joined the traffic department and became a relief crossing keeper, he was a very good gardener and won many prizes in local Horticultural Shows with his flowers, he was expert in growing dahlias among many others. Albert Hoare was older than the rest, and he retired from Wimborne. Albert had a brother, Ivor, who was a ganger on the Somerset and Dorset at Corfe Mullen, and who I was later to meet when I relieved there. Bert Haines was the last Inspector at Wimborne for the Permanent Way and after his retirement the post was not filled and the gangs then came under the jurisdiction of the Inspector at Bournemouth. Jim Howell, his office lad, then transferred over to the clerical grade and became a Booking Clerk at Wimborne, and when the station closed he went to a similar position at Bournemouth before taking early retirement.

The Signal and Telegraph Department were represented by the chief linesman, Charlie Rowe and an assistant, Ernie Prior. They were responsible for the maintenance of all the instruments, telephones and other electrical items in the signal boxes and offices from Wimborne to Hamworthy Junction, and could be called out to go anywhere at times. The services of these men were in constant demand, essential parts of the signalling system that should have been replaced long before were being 'patched up' and therefore prone to failure. Many of those failures would occur after the normal working hours and a message from the signalman that the linesmen were required somewhere or the other would necessitate my having to

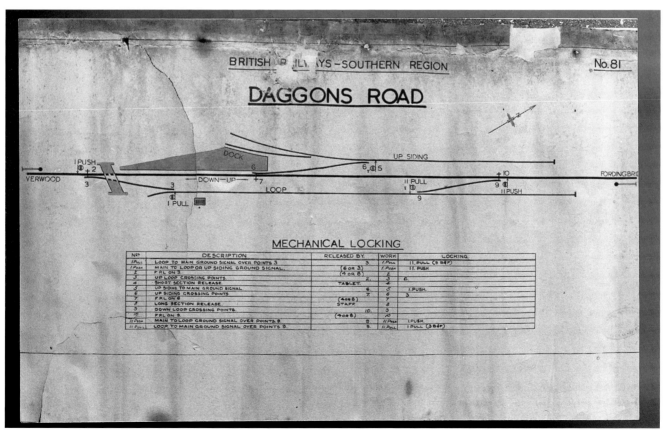

A brass oil lamp with the station name of Wimborne neatly written on a brass plaque.

make a hurried visit to his home.

I remember one evening on knocking the door of Charlie Rowe's house in Station Road, it was answered by his wife, who informed me that Charlie was not available and please go round and call out Ernie Prior. More or less the same thing happened when I arrived at Ernie's house in The Avenue, only this time his wife shouted down the hall, 'you in Ern?', 'no I'm not' came the reply, 'he's not in son' she said, 'go round and see Charlie Rowe'. I hadn't the heart to say that I'd already done that. In later years we became very good friends when I came to live in Wimborne, and I used to remind Ernie of when he wasn't in.

Two more members of the Signal and Telegraph were employed to look after the mechanical side of the job, points, signals, signal wires, crossing gates and the cranks and pulleys associated with all the workings, they were Ernie Sutton and Vic Fiford, Ernie was very deaf, ably looked after by his mate Vic when they were out on the line. Had it not been for the war it was certain that Ernie would not have been allowed anywhere near the running line being so deaf, but these were wartime days, and there was just no-one else to replace him. This very good partnership was tragically brought to an end when, whilst working on a signal close to the river bridge, Ernie was struck by the 7.00 a.m. train from Dorchester that used to terminate at Wimborne. Filled with remorse and completely devastated by the accident to his mate, I don't think that Vic Fiford ever worked again.

As far as I can recall the Carriage and Wagon Department had only one representative at Wimborne, Ernie

Mills. Ernie was responsible for seeing that all the carriages on the passenger trains and all the wagons on the goods trains that came under his scrutiny were fit to travel onwards, he also undertook to fill the axle boxes with grease or oil when required, and to carry out minor repairs that were within his scope, to vehicles that came to his notice during these routine examinations.

I have nearly omitted to mention the four guards that were based at Wimborne who worked goods and passenger trains and were graded accordingly, the two passenger men were Arthur Young and Charlie Bobbett, Harry Mills and Mark Middleton were the two goods guards. The passenger guards were rostered to work trains to Bournemouth West, Poole and Brockenhurst, the goods guards mainly to Hamworthy Junction, Poole and Dorchester South. Harry Mills was the first generation of a railway family and I have through my career worked with them all at some time or other. There were Harry's two sons Bill and Jack, Bill's three sons, Brian, Terry and Ricky, and Brian's son, Bobby. Harry would have approved of them all, Bill lived to a good age, sadly Jack didn't, and died somewhere in his fifties I believe. The remaining grandchildren are still carrying on a great tradition, it was my pleasure to have been associated with them.

Some of the people I recall being at the crossings, although I didn't know them at that time were Frank Gadd and Reg Shearing at Uddens, Frank Sansome and Bill Jeans at Canford, Bert Scrivens at Hayes Lane and this man Smith who did not take the office job at Wimborne was at Oakley. Frank Sansome at Canford had been a signalman but had an accident and lost a leg, and being unable to carry on with the signalling duties he was found this crossing keepers job at Canford. One of my duties in the Parcel Office was to sort out the stencilled notices advising of the running of trains that were not in the working timetable, in other words, 'specials'.

These notices were issued by the Divisional Offices at Southampton and sent to each station that the trains were booked to pass through. I would mark each one to where the notice had to go and the ones for the crossings had to be handed to the guards to throw out as they passed. It was not always possible for various reasons to contact each crossing by phone to advise them that a special notice was on its way, and if such procedure went unnoticed, they were at times caught unawares when a train suddenly appeared at their signal for which they had no knowledge.

Of course, it always happened as they had sat down for a meal or had closed the cabin and were on their way home. Coal for the fires and oil for the lamps were delivered either by a goods train which would make a special stop, or by lorry if the train had a heavy load on, water for drinking was conveyed in churns the same way. The crossing keepers were held responsible for maintaining the lamps in the signals and on the gates and generally keeping the cabin clean and presentable. A visit from the Stationmaster and Area Inspector once a week or so was never necessary to see that all was well. The cabins were always spick and span, floors polished, brasses shining, even the stove highly 'blacked'.

The crossing at Uddens was unique in that it could by turned into a signal box when required, in railway jargon, termed a 'block post'. *From Mondays to Fridays it would be required to come 'into circuit' at 7.30 a.m. until around 11.00 a.m. to shorten the section between Wimborne and West Moors for trains that were booked to run close to each other. On Saturdays throughout the summer it would remain in circuit until late afternoon or early evening to deal with the many holiday trains that ran just after the war ended.

It was also brought into circuit whenever a goods train was required to detach trucks of live cattle in the sidings of the Fatstock Marketing Corporation or to attach the empty cattle trucks after being unloaded, cattle and sheep were often detached from the first goods of the day, the 4.05 a.m. from Salisbury arriving just before 5.00 a.m. this siding was from the down line, on the up line was another siding, a much shorter one, holding about three wagons and was once for use of the occupants of Uddens House, a little way up Uddens Drive. Long since being required by them it was now used for loading away sugar beet to the Kidderminster factory of the British Sugar Corporation by farmhands of Trehane and Sons farm at Hampreston. *(I write of the Uddens that existed in 1955.)

Looking at the site of the old station today it is hard to realise that it all took place in so small an area, you could say that the station started almost from the end of the river bridge nearest Broadstone, alongside a short siding that backed on to a stop block and accessible from the up line was three wooden huts, one used by the Signal and Telegraph Dept., one by the Carriage and Wagon Dept,. and the last one by the Permanent Way Dept. Then came the up platform with, firstly, the Stationmasters office, then an empty room which I thought was possibly the tea room before the war (but one of my colleagues later thought not), then came a newspaper kiosk owned by W.H. Smith and Sons, railings guarding the steps to the subway, then came a door in the wall that had not been used for many years, and, what I believe to be the entrance from the Booking Office to the up platform when the station was built, from inside the office it would still have been possible to go up some steps and reach the platform when the station was finally closed but for this door which was well boarded up.

A ladies waiting room and toilet came next, a general waiting room, then a room used by the staff, always known as the 'porters room', then, side on, was a lamp room where all the signal lamps were stored and oil kept, plus an assortment of brushes, buckets, shunting poles and rubbish bins, next to that came the gents' toilets, and finally the signal box or lighthouse as it was known as. Twenty seven steps to the lever frame and a very good view of the surrounding area, I have often observed the arcing from the trolley buses in Bournemouth on a frosty morning, and the rising sun made a beautiful picture on a summers dawn.

The down platform started with a small 'bay' platform, which I understand was the one used for the Somerset and Dorset trains, but when I was there was used to berth overnight the stock used for a workmans' train that left at 5.17 a.m. to Southampton, this was later transferred to Hamworthy Junction. A general waiting room was at the end of that siding, the Permanent Way Inspector's office, then a small room next to that used for storing a number of cups, saucers, plates etc., which I presumed had come from the old tea room, though I still don't know where it originally was.

Then came the railings protecting the stairs down to the subway, a brick wall dividing the down platform from the number one road of the main marshalling sidings and goods yard, this at one time was another platform used by

A Southern standard signal and warning notice. At the time of this photograph in 1966, single line working was in operation.

trains making it what we termed as an 'island platform'. In the middle of this wall was a large sliding door and my lack of knowledge of the former layout made me wonder whatever this door was used for. I take it now that it allowed passengers access to the steps to the subway and out of the station. At the end of the wall was a ladies waiting room and toilet, finally a small gents toilet.

A small brick building off the end of the platform housed a weighbridge where wagons could be weighed in this forementioned number one road. Stations that had no weighbridge had to send wagons via Wimborne, advice of the tare, nett weight and gross weight would then be sent to that forwarding station either by phone or railway letter, this being another chore of the overworked goods clerk.

The siding accommodation stretched from the river bridge to Leigh Road, starting with, on the down side at the Broadstone end of the station the main yard consisting of eight roads, a road being a railway term for a set of lines used for shunting and/or stabling vehicles, usually ending with a wooden buffer called a 'stop block', protecting the end of that particular line. I suppose it would be right to say that all lines were known as roads, any reference made to them such as an enquiry as to what was about, say, on the up road, so that a shunt might be made not to delay anything, the word 'line' never came into it.

Numbers two and three roads were used to position

Above and below: The two Whitaker tablet catchers outside Corfe Mullen signalbox in 1965.

wagons for unloading and loading , number one road went from the river bridge to Leigh Road, and was joined at the West Moors end of the down platform by a pair of points leading from the down road. Once clear of the main line it was joined a few yards down by number two road, just beyond that a pair of hand operated points allowed a reversal into the goods warehouse and on to a stop block on the other side. Shunting on the down side created many problems at times, the points onto the main line had mostly to be open to allow long rows of wagons to be pulled up and shunted. Surprisingly there was no ground signal for a train to enter the yard from the main line, only to leave it, and so, when a train arrived it was the custom to operate the shunt signal that allowed them movements to go forward so that the shunter knew it was alright to come back.

There was two signals on the same post, the top signal allowed the driver to proceed on his journey, clearance for that being obtained from the Broadstone signalman. A warning bell was also provided to warn the shunter to vacate the main line as soon as possible to allow the passage of a train; if this was ignored, purposely or not, then the shunt signal would be replaced to danger and in busy times the tempers of train crew and shunters would be severely strained. The yard points, of course, could not be closed without the movement being clear of the running line and the warning bell acknowledged by the shunter.

Commencing with the up side accommodation, Poole siding, as it was termed, started from a set of points close to the end of the platform and ran back to a stop block close to the river bridge. In recent times this was used to berth overnight the first two push/pull sets out in the morning, the 6.22 a.m. to Brockenhurst and the 6.45 a.m. to Bournemouth West. At the other end of the station backing on to the signal box were two short sidings. The one nearest to the main line was called 'Salisbury' sidings, the next one to it was the cattle dock.

Salisbury sidings would be used to place parcels or goods vans, horse boxes and cattle trucks that had to be attached to passenger trains. Cattle pens were provided in the cattle dock for loading and unloading cattle and sheep to and from the market, access being from the market by way of a fairly steepish hill, and some of the methods employed to get the animals up or down that hill did not meet with my liking quite often when observing from the signal box. A single pair of points just ahead of the starting signal on the end of the platform led into both sidings, hand operated points were provided for whichever one was required.

Finally, two long sidings that stretched from Leigh Road bridge to within a few yards of the end of the platform, the road nearest the main line, number 1, was actually part of the cattle dock. It was possible to place some fifty wagons in each road, this was often the done thing when the 4.25 p.m. goods from Dorchester arrived in the early evening before going on to Eastleigh and the goods train to Salisbury was being made up. An earlier departure meant that preference was given and perhaps there was traffic on the Dorset goods for the Salisbury line.

The access to these sidings were not in the interests of safety of the shunter or the guard, the points leading in were operated by two levers in a small open ground frame, no ground signals were provided in or out, the method was that the shunter or guard, whoever was in charge of the movement, had to indicate to the signalman that the train was clear of the points by either waving his hands or, in the dark, his headlamp, above his head, or pressing a plunger above the two levers which would ring a bell in the signal box. The signalman would then pull an electrical release lever which would allow the release lever on the ground frame to be operated and the points opened. Mechanical locking in the signal box ensured that the starting signal leading towards that movement could not be pulled while the release was out in the frame, and that release lever could not be replaced until the one in the ground frame had been.

After making sure that the points were safe to travel over then the guard or shunter would have to walk along the down line to give the driver the signal either by hand or lamp to reverse back leaving himself open to getting run down if he wasn't very careful. There was a signal just round the corner from these sidings that allowed the train to continue on its journey, but not always with a long train was it possible for it to be within the signal and then it was up to the driver and the person giving permission to go to see that the signal was 'off' before starting. Many years ago there was a small siding on this curve which was used by the Wimborne Gas Works, but I saw no trace of it when I was there.

So much for sidings, what else do I remember about the station?

The cobbled forecourt which was still there at the station's demise, an old opening above it on the up platform which, I understand, was used for placing the passenger's luggage and the like on to the tops of the horse drawn coaches. The ancient custom of placing a rope across the

road each side of the Griffin Hotel, something to do with preserving an ancient right and prevented it from becoming a right of way, although I stand corrected on this issue, it all happened a long time ago, and, at that time it was only hearsay, I knew no history of it.

Next door neighbour to the station was a Billy Richards where one could find overnight accommodation after arriving late in the evening. Billy was a man of many talents, he delivered milk locally from a horse and trap, played in and led a dance band, and was a much sought after entertainer. Between his house and the station there was a path leading down to Leigh Road known by all as the 'Cinder path'. It served as access to the railway stables, the market and allotments on the side of the railway bank. Looking back as I do today it seems impossible that so much was crammed into so short a space, those yesteryear builders knew how. The two lines that ran from Oakley crossing to Broadstone is now a cycle track, I wonder how much land would now be required to turn it into a motorway.

Above: The round and square slots in the tablets were to prevent them being placed in the wrong instrument machine.

Right: Fordingbridge station in the early 1960s.

An impressive view of two Bulleid Pacifics at Bournemouth shed. 'West Country' Class No. 34032 *Camelford* dominates this picture. *Camelford* was never a Bournemouth allocated locomotive. Her last shed was at Salisbury where she lasted until October 1966 for withdrawal.

While enjoying my work my ambition to move to fresh fields had been fuelled by being allowed to ride on the shunting engines and occasionally on my way home to Branksome. I was by now something of a steam fanatic, fascinated by the magic of the engines I felt that my career lay in working on them, and so with this very much in mind, I sallied forth one afternoon to the locomotive sheds at Bournemouth to see the foreman and ask if there were any

A classic photograph of 'M7' Class No. 30031 complete with push-pull equipment, with an array of other Southern engines on shed at Bournemouth. No. 30031 was built in 1898 and was a long-framed version, being adapted to motor train operation quite late on in life. She was withdrawn in May 1963.   *W. Eccles*

Above: An unidentified Standard Class 4 prepares to depart for Southampton with a stopping train in June 1967. Most passengers appear to be waiting for an express for Waterloo on this beautifully sunny day. *Roger Hardingham*

Below: A famous member of the 'West Country' Class, No. 34016 *Bodmin*, sits in the yard at Bournemouth. Note the 'Quiet Please Residential Area' sign just behind the tender. This was to remind engine crews to keep down unnecessary noise as the depot was so close to housing.

Standard Class 4 Tank No. 80138 arrives at Bournemouth Central from the Poole direction. The line on the far right is a siding.

vacancies for young lads of my age. The reply was that 'yes, of course, there were many vacancies because of wartime shortages, but seeing that I was already employed with another department a written application would have to be made to the appropriate authority for a transfer'. What transpired next was to leave me saddened for much of my working life, I had not realised that I was part of what was termed 'a reserved occupation' and meant that I would not be called for military duties, only in extreme emergencies, and permission to transfer was hardly ever given. Men and women had been trained in essential railway duties, shunters, guards, drivers and firemen were irreplaceable, there was also many that, but for the war, would have been retired long before. My transfer request was turned down much to my bitter disappointment, I didn't understand how the work that I was doing came into the category of essential works, my contribution to the war effort of very little value. I had not realised then that I had been earmarked for training as a shunter elsewhere, and so join the ranks of these essentials, and so it wasn't long before it was decided that I

would move on and to Hamworthy Junction. On a day in April 1944 came a letter advising me to report to a Mr Brixton, the stationmaster there. Well, I had heard of the place but of it's exact location I knew not. I would miss Wimborne very much, all the friends that I had made, the routine that I had got into, I was to be a Junior Porter, whatever that was. Much apprehension began to set in. Maybe my arrival there would be to a somewhat hostile environment, or so I got to think, you know what sometimes can go on in a young man's mind when change is being forced upon him, and anyway, it wasn't my choice to go to Hamworthy Junction and so on and so on. The dreaded day duly arrived and at nearly the same time as I arrived at Wimborne eighteen months before, I arrived at Hamworthy Junction, perhaps a good omen, but there was no stationmaster to greet me as I arrived this time, I had to make my own way across to his office. I was to find out later that my arrival had coincided with the departure of Ken Newman, who was also joining one of H.M.Forces, as was the case at Wimborne.

Chapter Three
HAMWORTHY JUNCTION

Whoever had decreed at the Divisional Offices that this move should take place could not have known at the time that it would turn out to be in the best interests of my career, one of the times in life when the dice would roll and come up with the right number, and I remember my time served at Hamworthy Junction today with a great deal of satisfaction, affection for the place and its people, and all my colleagues among whom I was destined to spend some of the best days of my working life. I suppose that it wasn't surprising that for the first two weeks or so I wasn't very contented or enchanted with the place, and, but for some good advice from my father, I might have left but fate decreed otherwise and I stayed. Meeting Mr Brixton was somewhat of an experience, a tall, thin man, grey hair, of stern appearance, and I recall that here was a man who would not stand a lot of nonsense, and that it might be to my own good to knuckle down to a little more discipline than I had been accustomed to at Wimborne. Well, this turned out to be a good decision on my part. In later times he was to help my climb up the ladder as is said, quicker than I might have achieved elsewhere.

My first job was the same as the one that I did on arrival at Wimborne, make out the stock return, only this time compile it in the correct way, there were not so many wagons then a there were at Wimborne, and I learned of how it should be done after nearly eighteen months previous experience of the other way. The arrival of the Inspector Jock Habgood, causing no terrors now. Next on the roster was changing and cleaning signal lamps, a new experience for me. Some of the highest signals that I had ever seen were at Hamworthy Junction, and the prospect of climbing aloft with lamp in hand and hanging on to the small iron ladder for dear life with the other did not appeal to me very much, and a cigarette had to be lit before an ascent was attempted. Once up on the small wooden platform of the down starting signal, a panoramic view of Poole and Upton was bettered nowhere, and when I eventually overcame my apprehensions I quite enjoyed my

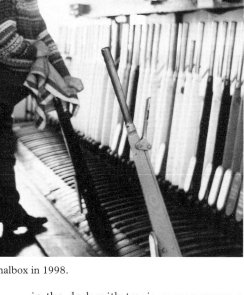

The author at the levers in Hamworthy signalbox in 1998.

excursions aloft, the only one that I was none too happy with was the down branch home signal on the single line from Broadstone, the reason for that was that it leant over at a precarious angle on the bank overlooking Lord Llewellyn's Upton house drive, and was not very steady anyway.

I was once hit on the side of the head while changing the lamp in the up starting signal, not quite so high as the down starter, but with a larger wooden platform to accommodate two signals side by side, the one for the main line (to Poole) being a few feet higher and reached by another short iron ladder. It was what was termed a 'four armed' post, two below and two high enabling the driver of a non-stopping train to see the signal well before it was reached, the approach being on a sharp curve, the left hand signal allowed entrance to the single line to Broadstone. On this particular day I had carried out the usual procedure in informing the signalman of my intentions, but it had gone clean out of his mind. Fortunately I received only a glancing blow and was able to get down to confront a very apologetic and remorseful signalman.

If the mail had to get through so had the lamps got to be changed, no matter what the weather, hail, rain, snow, or sunshine, if a lamp went out then there was a danger of a train going by in the dark with tragic consequences or worse. It was my practice to carry a small amount of methylated spirits and a lump of cotton waste to wipe off the iron steps before climbing them whenever the weather was bad, also handy for cleaning the red, green and yellow spectacles when snowed or frosted, not a job for the Winter months, but just right when it entailed walking across to Holes Bay on Summer mornings to change the down distant signal or down to Rockley Bridge to attend to the up distant.

Each morning around twenty to nine , an eight coach train would arrive from Wareham to be brushed out and door handles polished with pommedust; this would be the early morning train from Christchurch to Wareham, and locally termed 'the Holton Heath workman', it would then be berthed in Broadstone sidings before an engine off of one of the goods trains would take it back to Wareham to form the 5.17 p.m. to Christchurch, later returning to Wareham with the night shift and from Wareham to Christchurch with the late turn lot. This train had quite a chequered history attached to it. When it first arrived to take up these duties at Hamworthy Junction a first class saloon, complete with all the mod cons, had to be removed from the set and left for the rest of the war on the stop block in Broadstone sidings. Although I wasn't there at the time when it was taken away, Ron Gingell told me that a Carriage and Wagon examiner had a look round it, a drop of oil here and there and the brakes worked perfectly and off it went. They tell me that it was once one of the Ascot race sets of pre-war, it was also the train that was machine gunned by enemy aircraft one evening between Holton Heath and Hamworthy Junction.

Another train from Swanage would arrive about 1.40 p.m., this also needed brushing out and door handles polishing before berthing in Broadstone sidings for attention to the locomotive's fire etc., before departing at 2.40 p.m. back to Swanage. It was this train that provided the engine that I was to learn much about the art of taking water, cleaning and making up the fire, cleaning out the smoke box and generally preparing the engine for its next journey. With one particular train crew,who, as soon as I appeared on the scene, would hastily retreat to the Junction Hotel. When this happened it became my job to uncouple the train, take the engine forward, run round so that the engine was on the other end, pull forward and then place the train in one of the Broadstone sidings and carry on the good work before bringing it out again to the down platform ready to go with a full head of steam.

This little tank engine was one of the Adams 'T1' class No. 363, at frequent intervals it would have to go to Bournemouth for a boiler wash and whatever and then it was possible that an L11 tender engine would be sent or an M7 tank, mostly non push pull, commonly termed a 'Lever tank'. Whilst making a change, I preferred No. 363, and, of course, it remained my favourite engine.

I sometimes was allowed to take the controls of a 'B4' 0-4-0 tank engine that was berthed at Hamworthy Junction loco shed and used on the goods trains from there to Hamworthy Goods, the only engine that could negotiate the sharp curves in the sidings there and those on Poole Quay. 'Bugs' we called them, but weren't they a powerful little engine for their size and their age.

When I arrived in April 1944 there was a young man who started in 1943, name of Peter Bugler, 12 days younger than me, and we became very good friends and colleagues, our friendship existing to this day, we were to share in many happy hours while together, not to mention a few scrapes in which we were able to help each other out of, we also held a common liking of speedway at Poole Stadium on Monday nights, and many little wangles were arranged so that we were there when the tapes went up.

Hamworthy Junction was always considered, as I was to learn in later years, a good place to start, and I soon found out that I had the best tutors that existed anywhere, enriched by the arrival of a man who was to remain a great friend up to his untimely demise after retiring through ill health

fourteen years earlier, I say untimely, he was seventy seven but I have missed and often think of him, his name was Ron Gingell. Ron arrived a short time after me, and had previously worked on Salisbury Plain at Amesbury, Bulford, and Newton Tony, enduring many of the hardships, weatherwise, that the hostile plain could provide, he was to replace another shunter who had lost a leg in an accident while shunting the morning empty stock of the Holton Heath workman train, this happened in the week before I arrived. The unfortunate victim was George Craven who later went to Bournemouth Goods Junction as a signalman.

The staff employed at that time were the two signalmen, Harry Fall and Alfie Compton, shunters Ernie Bryant, George Witts, Clarrie King and Ron Gingell. Two grade 1 porters, Fred Carter and Jack Isaacs, and, of course, Peter Bugler and Mike Webb, me. Also attached to the station for payroll purposes were the Permanent Way Department represented by Sam Vallance, the ganger, his son, Stan Vallance, Jim Payne, Harry Rose who took over the gangers job when Sam retired, and the crossing keepers son at Lychett crossing, Arthur East. The locomotive department was also represented by drivers, Billy Bishop, who was graded as the foreman driver and was responsible for the Depot in the absence of a foreman as it was a sub depot of Bournemouth, George Oliver, Harry Agate and Jessie Sherrard. Firemen Sam Turner, Bill Hayward, Doug Scott and Fred Norman are the men that I remember.

Bill Bishop was very hard of hearing but seemed to have a feel of the engine somehow, in the times to come Bill would not have been allowed anywhere near a running line, but, once again, it was wartime and he had proved to be more than capable of doing his job. I remember thinking that it was possible that he heard more than you thought he could. He was one to conserve coal on the engine and would admonish his mate; more often than not that would be Sam Turner, for putting too much in the firebox. Sam would make some cryptic remark aside to me about his saving coal and I only had to watch Bill looking the other way with a quirk on his face which left me wondering if he had heard. It taught me not to say anything untoward about him in his presence.

To complete the complement of locomotive department employees at Hamworthy Junction, a coalman was employed overnight to generally prepare the two locomotives for the next day workings, unload the coal wagons on to a wooden stage, fill and trim the lamps and fill the oil cans, any time left was spent sprucing up the footplates and outsides of the locomotives. In 1944 this job was filled by Joe Day who lived in the Railway Cottages opposite and, who on his retirement, was replaced by 'Jocky' Whale, son of a pre-war signalman, and also living in the Railway Cottages having previously been employed at Kinson Pottery firing the brick kilns.

As at Wimborne it seemed a small place for the amount of work that went on there, mostly freight, but soon after the war ended empty trains that could not be dealt with at Bournemouth were diverted to Hamworthy Junction for cleaning, watering and berthing, many times for a day, before returning to wherever they came from. This meant some overtime money being paid out to most of us, even the signalmen were drafted in when the going got a bit hectic. Being situated where it was, it was a transfer yard for traffic

Ivatt tank No. 41312 runs bunker first at Corfe with a service from Wareham to Swanage. This engine is one of those preserved and operates on the Mid-Hants Railway as well as other lines periodically.

received from Portland, Weymouth, Dorchester, the Swanage branch,which would include many trucks of clay from the mines in the Corfe Castle area, and Hamworthy Goods. The many destinations were routed via the old road, (Wimborne/Ringwood), the Somerset and Dorset, Templecombe and Bath, and the main line to London and stations thereto.

There was in the heyday of goods traffic on the railway twenty-four trains that either called or terminated or started from Hamworthy Junction. Again, as at Wimborne, there was a weighbridge, and that was situated in number four road which could only hold about four wagons at any one time. This was the main shunting yard of four roads which was on the Holton Heath side of the station, two sidings, the long and the short docks were reached by a reverse movement from the yard and wagons destined for these two sidings and out again had to be what we called 'Fly shunted' or run off. This entailed the engine going at a fast rate forward, just a touch of the brake to allow the coupling to be dropped, and then changing the points (by hand) after the engine had passed over to get the wagon where you wanted it to go. This could be a hazardous occupation for the inexperienced, often a derailment would occur when the space between engine and wagon was insufficient, it was always better for two of you to attempt it although not always possible. I quickly

learnt not to operate the points unless there was plenty of room to allow me to do so. This sometimes meant that the wagon would follow the engine and then it would mean having another go, not always to the liking of the driver if he was wanting to get away.

I had just 'passed out' for shunting by the Area Inspector, Vic Rook, and the next day, a Tuesday, with the help of a driver, Ron Sansome. who was keen to get back to Bournemouth a shunt had to be made to place a wagon from the short dock into the weighbridge road for weighing. I wasn't too happy about doing it, not because I felt incapable, but that the head shunter whose mate I was, Ernie Bryant, was not there. 'Come on nipper' said Ron, 'I'll shout when it's alright to uncouple', and so it was, a perfect job, my first run off under my own steam so to speak, but when I next saw Ernie and told him that the job was done he went spare, 'don't ever do that sort of thing again without that I'm there', he said. Well, on the Thursday the position was reversed, Ernie had to do it on his own, and, as you might have guessed, yes, the wagon became derailed. He didn't live that one down for a long time, his older mates retorting, 'the nipper's better at it than you are Ern', though you will understand that I kept pretty quiet about the whole affair and anyway it soon blew over and we became great friends and mates after.

Ivatt tank No. 41320 is seen in these views at Wareham station. In the view above, it prepares for another service down the branch line to Swanage. In the photograph below, it runs round its train ready to return to Swanage.

I have gone on a little bit, before all that happened I was to become a grade 1 porter in the Booking Office, but only temporarily. Two good teachers, Fred Carter and Jack Isaacs instilled in me the workings of Railway Accountancy etc., and once again I was in direct contact with the passengers and our customers, and gaining a wealth of experience which would stand me in good stead in the months to come. Fred Carter was what was termed at that time, a grade 1 porter signalman, which meant that he was required to work in the signal box for a time not exceeding half the normal time worked by a full signalman, he mostly worked when the early turn man finished until the late turn man came on around four o'clock. I found him a hard taskmaster but very fair and understanding. If I came into the office on a cold morning and said that I was cold he would start punching me about the body saying that he would soon warm me up, my lesson was to be always nice and warm, but as he would always feel my hands to see if they were cold, I used to warm them up by the porter's room fire before putting in an appearance in the office.

Before the war there was a small cigarette machine on the platform, the property of the B.A.C., the British Automatic Company, and for some reason, while the machine no longer existed they still sent packets of cigarettes at regular intervals and entrusted with the selling of these was Fred. Peter and I, among others, would have a packet or two on the slate, paying our debts on a Thursday, pay day, which Fred always saw to it that we did.

Jack Isaacs worked opposite to Fred and was a different character altogether, he was also a bit younger. Where there was a little jiggery pokery going on then you could bet Isaacs was at the back of it somewhere. He took my bicycle to pieces one evening a few minutes before my train home was due, and put it on top of an old air-raid shelter just inside the fence at the end of the up platform; and then late one afternoon he asked me to accompany him home to Sandy Lane at Upton but gave no reason. On arrival there I was introduced to his wife, Hilda, and after a cup of tea I soon found out the reason for my presence, Jack wanted to take a

tandem back to the station to work on and I was to be the back seat rider. Never having ridden a tandem I thought it was good that we had reached Station Terrace and turned the corner to go up the rise when, half way up, the machine came to a sudden halt and we both came off, 'what's the matter mush', I asked, 'well I thought you was pedalling', 'I got a bit tired' was my answer. Yes, there was only one more to overcome after one got by Isaacs and you would only meet him in Hades.

Let's get back to commerce, we had a few customers that used the yard at Hamworthy Junction, Beacon Hill Brick Company loaded away trucks of clay, chiefly to the potteries area, Stoke on Trent, Burslem, Eritreia consigned to a J. Johnson, who was known to visit us occasionally to thank the staff for making out his accounts and rendering same; trucks of clay from Doulton's claypit on the Hamworthy Goods branch were sent in batches of five trucks daily to their depot at Belvedere in Kent. Trucks of coal were received for the Hooper Brothers, Charlie and Fred, joined after the war ended by Fred's son Henry. Kinson Potteries had their own small siding adjacent to their works and received regular supplies of coal for their kilns. Wallis Tin Stamping Company loaded away wagons of scrap tin to Llanelly in South Wales and sometimes a wagon of metal filings were loaded by staff of the George Cohen Group.

Being heavy material the wagons were always, when possible, placed in the short dock which was a lot lower than the roadway and so much easier to load. Once again it was my job to fetch the weighbridge book and bring it back each day to the office, only this time it was also my job to advise the various stations of the weights recorded therein. If I remember rightly, the charge for each wagon weighed being about ten pence.

Our passenger train service roughly amounted to about one an hour, plus about ten trains that were not booked to stop; busy really when the goods trains that ran were taken into account, plus all the empty stock trains that arrived and departed. Busy or not, there was always time for a little bit of boyish mischief to go on as you might expect

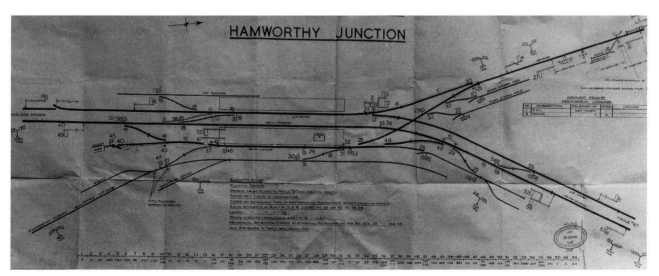

The signalling diagram from Hamworthy Junction showing the lines to Broadstone and Poole on the right and the line to Holton Heath and the Hamworthy Goods line on the left.

when two lads get together, and Pete Bugler and I were no different from the rest.

A goods train, the 12.06 pm from Dorchester, would arrive daily just before 3 o'clock and every now and then a regular Dorchester crew would be on board. Now Peter and I had observed that it was the practice of the driver to get off the engine and leave his mate to do the shunting. Harry Blandemere was the driver and his fireman, one of the oldest at Dorchester in those days, was Ernie Batchelor, in fact they were both grey haired and at first it was hard to know who was the driver of the two. One afternoon Peter decided that it might be a good idea to place a large can of water above the porters room door and view the result from a safe distance, however, much to our horror, it wasn't Harry that got off, it was Ernie, and of course he walked straight into it. This wasn't at all what we had planned, for Ernie looked to be a bit of a handful and we both didn't fancy getting tangled up with him. He looked around the station for a considerable time, or so it seemed to us, and we had to keep well out of sight until he went back to the engine a little damp, and more than a little annoyed.

Came the next day, Peter and I once again taking our place of refuge, we observed Ernie to get off the engine with a bucket of very filthy water, the porter's room door being slightly ajar, he saw someone sitting inside, the window looking out on to the road was open, so he quietly walked round and without looking threw the water through the window, all over one of the guards sat making out his train journals, Nobby Clarke. Now Nobby was not very happy, train journals washed out and spoilt, wet through and in a bit of a state himself, he knocked on the stationmaster's door, it was his half day off. Now providence can sometimes be very cruel but to us it showed a great deal of mercy on this day, he wasn't in. He hardly ever went out on his half day, but on this particular day he was. By the next day Nobby had cooled down and saw the funny side of things, and did not pursue the matter further,but it didn't end there.

Having got away with that little lot we decided to take the carriage watering hosepipe and stretch it from the hydrant on the down platform, across onto the roof of the up platform, where we lay in wait for their arrival, making sure that our ladder to get down was safely on the roof. They arrived, we got them and when we tried again later in the week they were prepared and were tucked in well into their cab so that our efforts were in vain. Several skirmishes followed, more people got involved, and it was only through the good offices of friends down the line who told us when our two adversaries were on the engine, that we managed to dodge a soaking.

I well remember one incident that occurred one afternoon, I had issued a young lady a ticket to Holton Heath and walked round with her to the down platform and stood talking to her, when, as the engine passed us, a paper bag full of water whizzed by my head and hit the advertising board behind the young lady and me, she getting most of what came out of the bag, I cannot recall what the outcome of it was, but I heard no more about it, lesson learnt?, not on your life, these water games went on to the day that I left to join the Army at the end of 1946.

A sad story to relate now, and one that taught me a lesson, for was I not the same as the rest when it came to dealing with people that had suffered nervous breakdowns and had not fully recovered. One such person was a Michael Docherty, though his surname might not be right, it was a long time ago. It gives me no pleasure whatsoever to recount what follows, only a deep sense of regret and a wish that I could have been more understanding.

Michael came to us, invalided from the R.A.F., and was on the railway prior to joining up I believe. To two young lads it was all hilarious. In the mental state that he was left in he would complain that a whispering campaign was going on and that there were voices coming from anywhere and everywhere. Of course, Peter and I would carry it further by suggesting that they probably came from under the signal box among many other places, and we did nothing to ease his fears only taking the 'mickey' as they say. However, one morning Michael accompanied me across to Broadstone sidings where there was stabled over a hundred wagons out of position waiting acceptance by Hamworthy Goods whose sidings were hopelessly congested and could only accept ones or twos at a time as well as the traffic that arrived daily from where the trains for them were made up.

It was our job to compile a list weekly that would show the wagons and contents and consignee's still on hand waiting acceptance. We had made a start when suddenly it came on to rain and I decided that we should shelter under a wagon until the worst had passed over. We sat, one on each axle and then it was that Michael started to talk to me. It was as if he was now in command of all his senses, the first real intelligent conversation that had passed between us, and it was of one incident that was to affect him for the rest of his all too short a life.

I was completely enveloped in his account of a R.A.F. fire tender chasing along the runway after an aircraft that was on fire and on nearly coming to a standstill it blew up in a ball of flame. The intense heat prevented the firecrew, of which Michael was a member, from rescuing the men inside, the pitiful cries of the stricken men had not left his mind, he had always felt guilty of not being able to go in and get them out. This was the first and last time, as I have said, that I ever had any form of conversation that I understood with Michael, and sadly he was unable to cope with his experience on on the fire tender and left the railway to die shortly afterwards. I said at the start that I learnt a lesson, I did. Never again did I ever treat anyone with any nervous disorder in the way that I did Michael. It is always good when one is young to learn a lesson that will stay with you for the rest of your days, and Hamworthy Junction seemed to be the best place to be taught.

I became aware of a Charlie Dominey, stationmaster at Hamworthy Goods, and I also became aware that he was a 'no good so and so' as labelled by my own stationmaster, Harry Brixton. For some reason there was not a lot of love lost between them, especially when it came to dealing with those wagons held in Broadstone sidings. Charlie would ring up and ask for certain wagons to be included on the next available goods train that were possibly right on the end, close to the stopblock, this meant that a whole string of wagons had to be pulled up, took across to Poole sidings, these certain wagons took out and the rest replaced, time and opportunity did not always fit and so Charlie was told in no uncertain manner that he would get what came,like it or lump it. This, of course, led to bitter rows and Harry had been known to bang the phone down calling upon the powers to be to rid him of this troublesome character who wanted everything his way. This opinion rubbed off on me, and I was soon to learn how wrong that sort of thing can be.

As I have mentioned before, the job that I was doing was only temporary, and as such, I was available to cover anything that cropped up both at the Junction and the Goods, and one afternoon the number taker went sick at the Goods and I was asked to relieve him until he came back. That boy, Brian Tarrant, a Clerical Officer at Wool, turned out to be a very good friend of mine to this day, had contracted chicken pox. What to do about this 'ogre' of a man, Charlie Dominey? I couldn't sleep the night before, filled with fear and trepidation at meeting this awesome man with a reputation of a devil.

Within an hour of arriving I began to realise that everything I had been led to believe about the occupants of Hamworthy Goods was quite wrong. On my arrival I was introduced to the occupants of a small office in the building that was once part of the original Poole Station in 1847, sitting at one end of a long desk much like the one in the office at Wimborne, was a lady clerk whose name is shrouded in the mists of time, next to her was a Ken Greenstock, chief clerk, commuting each day from Swanage. 'So you are Michael', said a round faced, bespectacled portly figure, almost saintly in appearance I remember thinking. I assumed that this had to be that Mr Dominey, this almost devil that I had heard about, 'yes sir, I am he' I replied, 'well, I know that you know what to do but in addition to that Brian went down to Newmans boatyard to get the cocoa and that is what I would like you to do if you will about ten o'clock'. 'Can't say I know where this boatyard is sir,' I said, 'Don't worry, come in when it's time and I will accompany you there'.

The appointed hour arrived and off we both went, me with a large jug in hand, I was introduced to the ladies behind the counter in the canteen as the lad replacing Brian, until he came back from the chicken pox. The large jug of cocoa was in addition to some gorgeous dripping sandwiches which I shared on our arrival on a cold morning back in the goods office. Mr Dominey also arranged for me to have dinner in the canteen of the timber firm opposite, J.T. Sydenhams, and I felt very high and mighty sat next to a stationmaster and to one of the 'high ups' of the timber firm. I had not paid a penny either for the cocoa or dinner, this was paid for by Mr Dominey, I had come unprepared, money wise, for such hospitalities, this was remedied for the rest of my stay there.

My experience in his domain was that no-one could have done a better job under extreme circumstances, sometimes restricted by being unable to get the wagons from Hamworthy Junction that was required, perhaps urgently, by some of his traders. In this day and age he would have made an excellent public relations officer for some firm, his relations with the top people of the firms that were catered for by the Southern Railway were superb. J.R.Woods, The Cement Marketing Board, James Bros., J.R.Smith's, J.T.

Sydenhams, Carter Tiles Ltd., are those that I recall. It certainly was a busy place in those days, sidings stretched from J.R. Smiths at Lake Road to J.R. Woods on Poole Quay, one of the sidings, Carter Tiles Ltd., were so sharply curved that horses had to be used to shunt them, in later years a tractor was purchased.

Ted Parsons was in charge of the horses, somewhat deaf, Ted treated his two horses like they were humans, I think they knew what to do before he ever hitched them up to a wagon. You could see them trotting on down on their own to the place where the points had to be turned, perhaps Ted helping his other mate, Charlie Coey, head shunter, to do another job in the meantime. Here was another character, Charlie liked his daily intake of ale and would disappear after signing on in the morning to help in the cleaning of the nearby Potters Arms and the Shipwrights Arms on the quay.

It was my job to shunt the first goods arriving in the morning around 7.30 a.m., Charlie re-appearing just before Mr Dominey came on about 8.30 a.m. For all his vices he was one of the best shunters of his day, I was present on one day when his recorded weights of wagons of coal sent out by J.R.Woods weighed as they moved over the weighbridge, were queried by the Manager of that firm, though I believe it was all in fun really. 'Right', said Charlie, 'tell you what, if I am a hundredweight out I'll give you ten bob, if I'm not then get your money out.' The procedure of weighing was gone through again, only this time each individual wagon was stopped on the weighbridge with the result that said Manager had to dip into his wallet for ten bob.

I was there the morning after a violent storm had taken place overnight, to find a flying boat washed up on the beach plus five motor torpedo boats and the whole of the ballast on the line next to the sea wall, washed away and it was not until the arrival of several wagons of ballast some days later that normal service could be resumed.

Another morning when I arrived I was greeted with the news that a Catalina flying boat had crashed the previous afternoon while trying to land a few yards from the shore. The cries of the crew trying to escape from the ensuing fire were heard by those that witnessed the accident from the shore, I believe that there were no survivors. Mr Dominey was very much affected by what he had seen and was pleased that he had let me go home a bit earlier the day before sparing me from a horrible experience.

Each wagon of cement received was double sheeted in the Winter to protect their contents from the weather, and another of my duties entailed helping another of the men employed there over retirement age to strip these tarpaulin sheets from each wagon, fold them up and throw them in a wagon before being sent away to wherever they might be required. Ted Wilkins was my mates name, a man of over seventy years old and still as strong as an ox, his strength amazed me. Together we folded and stowed away one hundred and twenty five of these sheets in a little under two hours, very hard work for a man of his great age, likewise for a nipper fifty years his junior.

I had reason to be grateful to my friends in the office as well, anything that I was not too sure about I could go and ask them and nothing was too much trouble. Brian came back after a fortnight off and it was with a tinge of sadness that I had to return to the Junction, a great deal more experienced having been privileged to work with and learn once again from people who were indeed experts in their profession. The lesson learnt from my visit was, never judge people by what you hear about them, you could be so wrong.

Another happening to further my education was after returning to Hamworthy Junction form somewhere on my travels, my great friend and confidant, Ron Gingell, told me of an incident that had occurred in my absence, a pay packet of one of the Permanent Way men had gone missing, which left all those people working in the office under suspicion. The govnor (Mr Brixton) knew his men well and knew that none of the regulars were capable of stooping so low as to take another colleague's money and so when a certain man came on duty he set a trap.

He asked this man if he had emptied the toilet monies lately, and if not please do it now. On inspecting the ticket book a short while later to sign everything as correct he noticed that not all the money that was in the box had been paid in, and asked the man to turn out his pockets, which he did, to reveal some marked coins that Harry had placed in the box. One minute's notice was the sentence, the gamble had paid off, a huge cloud was lifted from the rest of the lads, the railway police had not been called in, and no further action was taken.

I have remembered for all my working life that incident and have passed on to the young people, that I have been honoured to be involved in instructing, that to appropriate even half a penny of the company's money and you become immediately of no use to them, more than ever in this day and age when you are called upon to handle large sums of money, especially those issuing tickets on trains and elsewhere that one is in a position of great trust more so today than ever before, and honesty just has to be the best policy.

The war had ended in August 1945, a few of the men that had joined up from the railway were set to return but not all, we were joined by Tony Williams from Broadstone, and Alan Frampton, an evacuee from the Southampton area, soon to be christened by Ernie Bryant as 'Boo Boo', both were there to be trained as shunters. Things seemed to go on as before. Tony Williams nearly got himself killed when he jumped from the roof of the down platform and scooted off down Carters Avenue to dodge a bucket of water from Ernie Batchelor who proceeded down Carters Avenue after him.

Four lovely girls from number one Railway Cottages had to be regularly chatted up when we thought 'old Lurcher', as Peter had christened the stationmaster, wasn't looking. We came to agree that they were all 'smashers' as we said in those days, Madeline, known to all as Madey, Joan, Gloria and Thelma. Joan had lost a leg in a playground accident while still at school and would sit at the window while being chatted up by all the drivers and firemen who would get off their engines whenever the opportunity existed. Madey was later to suffer a very nasty nervous breakdown, at the time she was courting a young man from Bournemouth who waited for her to recover and then they were married. Gloria went away to London to work and met her future husband there. Thelma was later to marry Tony Williams and to the great surprise of all and sundry around

and abroad our confirmed batchelor and my own great friend Ron Gingell married Joan.

Meantime, my mate Peter had landed himself in a spot of bother with his arch enemy, 'old Lurcher'. I was in the office one morning when Harry Brixton came in and said, 'have you seen Bugler lately Michael?', 'no sir' I replied very truthfully, and with that he put on his hat and walked out of his office and made his way towards Poole along the down line. On arrival at the distant signal he found that Peter was making up for lost time and taking a short siesta in the morning sunshine. I supposed afterwards that Harry had been concerned that Peter might have been hit by a train or something, perhaps having observed him with a lamp in hand some little time previous, anyway, the outcome of their meeting was that Peter had to attend the Divisional Superintendent's office at Southampton to tender his explanation for his misdeed, and soon after he left Hamworthy Junction and went to Bournemouth, and I lost a good mate.

Replacing him was a young lad from Poole who worked on the W.H. Smith's newspaper kiosk on the station there, his name was Reggie Penfold. I remember the morning that he came asking about the vacancy, and Jack Isaacs in the signalbox came over and hid his bicycle in the up side gent's toilet, and that was Reggie's introduction to Hamworthy Junction, but he took it all in good part, though he must have wondered what sort of place it was when your bike goes missing and lands up in the toilet, and not a soul with any knowledge as to how it got there.

One afternoon I came out of the office on hearing the approach of the Micheldever goods, it having to be observed by me because it nearly always had an Austerity War Department engine on the front, and not too many of those ever reached Hamworthy Junction. It would be shunted by Tony Williams and Alan Frampton, I returned to my books and within a minute or so there was a devil of a bang from outside and my first thoughts were that there had been a crash on the main line. I ran outside onto the platform to see the train on the down line with just a few wagons attached and a cloud of dust coming up from the Broadstone sidings.

What had happened was that Tony had uncoupled a long string of wagons with the brake van on the end, the guard had got off and left Alan to deal with the braking back on to the stop block in Broadstone number one siding, Alan not taking into account the state of the rail, still a bit greasy in the shade of the trees that grew on the bank, misjudged the speed and when he eventually did put the brake on it was too late.

The wheels just picked up and went, the brake van went straight over the stop block, followed by a truck of coal that perched precariously on top of the block, lock buffered by the next one, the next two or three being derailed. The best part of all this was that Alan was in no way injured, he had jumped off the van before it went over the block and the single line to Broadstone was not affected. The incident proved to be a source of overtime for many of us, a mobile crane on an open wagon was sent down and members of staff were recruited to rerail the wagons.

This was normally a job for the motive power cranes, but in wartime days it was not considered important enough for them to attend, running lines not being fouled. I remember my stint with Fred Carter, more or less the blind leading the blind, as it is said. We both had no experience of where the chains should go round the wagon so that on lifting it would come up straight and not perhaps fall on to the running line, even placing the jib where it should go became a work of art, I cannot remember how long it took to clear it all up but I know that it was more than a week and the extra money was welcome.

I remember the day it was my good fortune to escape getting derailed, it happened when 'my' 363 had to return to Bournemouth to get attention to wheel flats caused when the driver omitted to reduce speed over a length of track on the Swanage branch that had recently been relaid. On realising his error he applied all brakes to reduce speed to the required twenty miles an hour, too late, the wheels picked up and flattened the tyres on all driving wheels. An old Adams 'L11' class tender engine was sent to replace it, but on arrival attached to the train that we were wont to attend to, it was found to require coal before the next journey was undertaken. To get to the coal stage in our small loco shed on your own, you had to jump off the engine before reaching a pair of points which were on a return spring and had to be held while the engine passed over, (alright with a small tank engine but not so good with a tender on behind,) and then you had to run and rejoin the engine to stop it right for taking coal.

It was better that two persons took part in this operation. Not ever having had to deal with a tender engine in this way I incurred the wrath of the fireman who would miss his beer time by my refusal to do it, and so it was he chose not to take me with him in this particular movement.

When next I looked towards the engine shed, I saw that the engine's two front bogie wheels were off the road (derailed), it being later found that the rails had spread with the weight on them of this engine not usually berthed there. It was a very severe curve from the entrance to the coal stage

and since only our two small engines ever went round there it was no surprise that this had happened, nobody ever remembers it being relaid. After all they may have been the same rails that were used when the shed was built many many years before, and wartime maintenance off the main line was almost non-existent.

On the first day of 363 being back in service we had been tipped off that the loco Inspector, Jack Hookey, would be arriving to see the driver concerned with flattening the wheels. Now Jack was a well known and well liked and respected man, but it did not do to let him see anyone that shouldn't be on one of his engines, and so Peter and I had to stand around and watch the fireman do what we usually did in the absence of any authority. Just as the engine passed the point where the two men stood in conversation, the rod that holds the brake blocks connected to the two driving wheels snapped and ripped up part of the wooden crossings at the Poole end of the station, throwing up stones and broken pieces of timber all over the place. Jack is reported to have said, 'well mate, it was a good job I was here and saw it all or you might have got the blame for this lot as well.'

As well as being acting engine drivers Peter and I were fairly good signalmen, well educated by the two resident men, Harry Fall and Alfie Compton, but even that had its pitfalls. I was in the company of Alf one late afternoon and accepted a train from Poole whilst he was having a snack, I had then to set the road for the accepted engine to run into the loop line. It was the custom for it to replenish the tender with water at the column at the Wareham end of the down platform, which could only be reached via the loop. I couldn't have taken a lot of notice of what I was advised was on the way, (there are different codes of bell signals for different types of trains,) because when I looked up on hearing a whistle there was the fast (non-stop) 1.30 p.m. from Waterloo to Weymouth approaching, probably wondering why this unusual diversion. I was flummoxed and appealed to Alfie for help, 'Oh no mister' he said, 'you got yourself

Lever labels from Bournemouth West Jct.

into it, now you get yourself out of it'.

Well after a couple of minutes had passed I managed to work out the route by studying the diagram above the frame, by which time I had caused a few minutes delay to the train which my mate had to answer for. I don't know how he got round it, for my actions were quite illegal, against the rules and regulations for anyone not 'passed out' by the Inspector, and, anyway, I was only 16 at the time.

Another breach of the rules I recall being committed by a lady who came to the window one dinner time to buy a ticket. This brought a most distasteful side of railway work to my notice and at such an early age. It happened like this. The lady, who was accompanied by an older woman and pushing a large pram, asked for a return ticket to Manchester producing a Forces Paybook, production of which a reduction in fares was allowed. There was no printed tickets from Hamworthy Junction to Manchester, no call for such an item I suppose, well, no regular call anyway, and I had to look the fare up in a book before writing a ticket out. Try as I might I couldn't find a fare to Manchester listed in our book, and told the lady that I could only book her to London and she would have to get another ticket there. 'But I only had one from here about a month ago' she replied. As all tickets that are written out are recorded in what was called the Blank card book, I looked through that for the month previously and the month before but found no record of issue.

Mr Brixton, who was in his office had heard all this going on and came into my office, and asked what the problem was. I told him and the whole rigmarole was gone through again, after which he told the lady that there was no way that she had purchased a ticket from this station to Manchester, it must have been from Poole perhaps which the lady accepted as possible, she must have forgotten. I then issued her a reduced fare ticket to London and that was the end of that. However, about twenty minutes after her train had gone, Mrs Brixton came out to tell me that Harry had jumped up from the table while eating his dinner and made off down the road on his bicycle, something to do with a ticket she said.

The mystery was solved when he came back some time later. After the train had gone he had observed this lady to pass his window still pushing the pram, but minus the other person, and Harry had assumed that the ticket we had issued at a reduced fare had illegally been given to to this other person, and he had been right, the other person was the lady's mother.

Some short time afterwards a member of the Railway Police came to see me and said that I would have to attend the Magistrates Court at Poole to give evidence against the lady for allowing a reduced fare ticket to be used by a person not entitled to such a ticket. I was filled with much apprehension about going to court. In the first place I felt sorry for the lady in that she could not have had a lot of money, being a serviceman's wife, and secondly her mother was living in Manchester and perhaps could not afford to come down very often. As it worked out on the day, I was not required to stand in the witness box, a plea of guilty was entered but, she was fined a large sum of money for her offence, and I felt at the time that she was held up as a lesson to others not to try the same or else. Nevertheless I did feel sorry for her at the time and hoped that never again would I get involved in a similar case.

'West Country' Class No. 34104 *Bere Alston* is about to pass under Dorset Road Bridge on its way to Weymouth.

Chapter Four

ON RELIEF

It was now 1946 and my job in the office had to be given up to a returning serviceman, Dick Northover. Dick came from a railway family who lived near the end of Carters Avenue, his father was at the Junction pre-war, but had been sent to Portsmouth as a shunter but, because of the bombings there, he would not let his family join him, he was always to be known as 'Old Dick', his son as 'Young Dick'. In later years he would return to Poole as shunter prior to retiring. Another of his sons, Ray, joined the railway later at the Junction and he was shunter for a while before getting married and going to London as a guard.

This left me surplus to requirements and I was asked if I would fill in with some relief work, which I agreed to. My first assignment was a stint of eight weeks more or less late turn at New Milton, twelve hours, nine to nine, which played havoc with any social life that I might have had. My duties consisted of once more attending to the signal lamps, general portering on the platform and assisting in the small goods shed when required. Twice a day, one on the up road and one on the down, a goods train would stop at the platform and we would have to unload goods destined for New Milton, this was known as 'road boxes' in railway jargon. My two colleagues, one on each turn early and late, were Tom Ansty and Alfie whose surname once again has vanished from my memory in the mists of time. They were both close to retiring at that time and I tried to do as much of the heavy work as I could to save them having to, they were both very nice people and I seemed to hit it off with them very well.

I enjoyed my stay, met a lot of nice people, came across Harold Silverthorne again, who I mentioned was at Wimborne for a time. There was also a very nice young lady working in the booking office, about my age too. I found out that she lived at Walkford but that was all that I ever did find out about her. A lot of servicemen returning from the Middle East at a local wartime airfield would arrive to catch a train, some carrying bananas, a commodity that had been missing from the shelves for many wartime years. The main problem for me at New Milton was the hours that I had to do, to make them longer my train home would often be running late, meaning that I could be away from home comforts sometimes sixteen or seventeen hours a day and that when I was starving hungry was a long time.

One night, no sign of the train, I decided to rough it and cycle home. I lived in Alder Road, Branksome, at the time. Not sure of which direction to take I made enquiries of my mate, Tom Ansty, and he directed me, 'turn right out of the station, then right again at the silent policeman.' Now in ignorance of what a silent policeman was, I took it to be a pub which was greeted with much hilarity when I arrived next day. Naturally I never did find one of that name, but I got home in the end. Took me longer than I bargained for though and I never tried it again.

The train that I came up on in the morning was the one that a certain young lady caught each day to New Milton from Bournemouth with her bicycle as she had some little way to go to the place where she worked. Being one of the

regulars she would be well known among the guards of that day, and one morning a guard from Bournemouth West, a Dickie Place, decided that he would be letting down her tyres, when the door was opened to let her out. The train arrived, the door opened, the lady stood aghast at seeing her front tyre was being let down. Dick was full of apologies, he would not have done it if he thought that he would have been caught doing this dastardly deed. The lady was furious, 'take me to the stationmaster', she said and the train went on. The next morning she came with said bicycle to the van and there stood the culprit, 'Guard', she said, 'I've got an apology to make to you', 'Oh', said Dick, 'yes', she said, 'I pushed that bike for nearly a mile and a half before I discovered that the wretched tyre was not flat at all', laughter all round and she took it all in good part.

The next station that I was required to go to was the next one down the line, Hinton Admiral, not a happy place for me, most of the time I was on my own, not knowing the routines and not being told by another member of the staff who was a regular relief man, I don't think that he was very pleased to have me there, a young temporary whippersnapper, still with napkins on my backside. I came into conflict with the signalman as well during a shunting move in the absence of my senior colleague. Wagons off the up goods train had sometimes to be placed in the sidings on the down side and there was a way of doing this, adhering to local rules for just such a move.

I decided that I would do it my way, give the signalman the necessary hand signal to alter the points from the up line to the down. Having seen that the points were set and safe to pass over, I uncoupled the wagon and relying on the handbrake to stop it, which I did almost opposite to the signal box. The official way was to bring the whole movement over with the engine attached, secure the wagon, and return to the up line to continue shunting. It could be that this move had to be made more than once if wagons were not marshalled as they should have been, quite often the case. Anyway, my way was quicker but the signalman thought otherwise.

Apparently a little time before this move had taken place, someone had missed the brake and some part of the train had run away down the bank (incline) into Christchurch. Mercifully no trains were in the vicinity at the time and a tragedy was averted. I had no idea that this had happened but my signalman made it clear in no uncertain terms that he was allowing no such a thing to happen again and the job had better be done the right way or else, and it was.

Have you ever been to somewhere where you are aware that your face doesn't fit? The next station that I had to go to was that place, Brockenhurst, I met people there that I knew at once that I wasn't going to get on with, and again the rosters demanded that I do a late turn for much of the time. One of the Station Inspectors was a man that I would meet up with again some years later at Dorchester, his name was Leslie Harris. His opposite mate was a Jack Damen. Les

'Merchant Navy' Class Pacific No. 35024 (soon to be named *East Asiatic Company)* at Boscombe with the 11.57 'up' stopping train on 27th November 1948. This locomotive was just 14 days in traffic when this photograph was taken, which means that this train was probably a running-in service. It received the 'blue' livery at Brighton Works the following March and was rebuilt in 1959.   *G. Pearce*

was sympathetic to my protests about late turn all the time, Jack was not, and one day I was invited into the Stationmaster's office to air my views on the subject. I was told to get on with the job or I'd find myself out on the street, so, as you might guess, Jack and I did not exactly hit it off, and I did my utmost to keep out of his way. To add injury to insult (I know it's the other way round really but it fits in better) I burnt my hand when I was there one morning while uncoupling an engine from a train, and omitting to turn the steam heating valve off enough. It was a naughty thought I know but there was an explosion in the basement of the Station Buffet one morning, hurting one of the ladies in charge, and I remember thinking that it was a pity that it was not the station that had gone up, I know that I couldn't get away from Brockenhurst quick enough.

My stay was for about a month and then I was required to report to the Stationmaster at Boscombe, what to do I didn't know until I got there. What a difference, I met the legendary Tommy Reed, a man well liked and respected by everyone that knew him. I too became full of admiration for the man, one of the finest Stationmaster's of his day, and even now I feel very pleased that I knew him and I was to meet him again when he ended up at Wareham, and I was again to come under his wing in my first signalman's position at Holton Heath, but that was to be in the future then. I was told that the job I had been sent to do was hard

work, unloading mail bags from covered vans into a lorry owned by Pardys, the furniture removers, specially hired, or perhaps commandeered, for the job.

My companions in this task were Italian prisoners of war, and only one spoke a smattering of English, so that, as you may imagine, conversation was somewhat limited and it was me that could understand a little Italian at the end, not them any English. I thought at the time that they were not overworked or underfed although their freedom might be a bit restricted. They had regular breaks and meal times were of the same length as me and were treated very well considering their status. One evening, after a long day, Tommy came over and said that I may go home early as we were more or less 'squared up'. I had my bicycle on the up platform and on reaching there I looked down the line to see a train just leaving Pokesdown.

Lunch bag over shoulder, coat over handlebars, I sped down to the wooden crossing at the end of the platform and three parts across off I cam, straight over the handlebars. Picking myself up I still made the train but in a lot of pain. I got off at Branksome and had to leave my cycle on the station, no way could I ride, and no way could I push it. It was snowing and I had just over a mile or so to walk, which I did with great difficulty, knocking my painful arm at one point on the way. I couldn't bear anyone to touch me and my Father undressed me with great caution, cutting one of my

Bulleid 'West Country' Class No. 34009 *Lyme Regis* approaches Gas Works Junction tender first *en route* to Bournemouth West.

garments to get it off, my vest I think. A visit to Poole Hospital next morning confirmed that I had a badly dislocated shoulder, many cuts and bruises to the arms and legs.

After treatment, (that was painful as well) I was off work for a week, and then, of all things, I was back to loading mails this time loading at Bournemouth Central.

Several covered vans were positioned in the bay siding at the London end of the up platform and used for conveying parcel mails that would be attached to a special train later in the day. My knowledge of where bags of mails were routed via was not very good. Vans were chalked up with different destinations, and it was my job to put them in the particular van where they were labelled. I had a mate, Bill Bennet, and when he chose to leave me to it, which was often, many of the mails with destinations that I was unsure of the route they should take, went in the 'London' vans.

I cannot now remember why, but it was my misfortune to have to attend the Stationmaster's office having committed some misdemeanour or other, and, on entering this holy of holies, I was commanded by the chief clerk that my hat be removed in his presence. Mr Nobbs was his name as was the S.M., but not related. Well, I had never had to undergo this sort of treatment when hauled before a Stationmaster before, and not ever having seen a lot of him either before, I didn't like the look of him anyway, I wish I could remember what it was all about, but it did not go down very well I recall and I wasn't long at Bournemouth.

I'll bet the authorities that be at Southampton didn't go

a bundle on my now increasing disciplinary record, interviews at Brockenhurst and now at Bournemouth and still only eighteen years old, what next they must have thought. I survived, but it must have been touch and go, because at eighteen no-one was going to push me around or so I thought.

Branksome was the next port of call and provided some very happy hours, I was upgraded there to a grade 1 porter as I was when leaving the Junction, and my opposite mate on the other turn was a very nice middle aged lady, Ivy Lillington, whose brother had taken over the Stationmaster's position at Wimborne from Mr Carter when he retired. Ivy was a very competent lady, excellent at figures and was often called upon to correct the mistakes of a not so competent booking clerk, not very well gifted in railway accountancy or even adding up figures. Owning quite a high pitched voice in my teens, she had christened me 'Squeaker', and I was delighted when one day she told someone that Squeaker was the only one that, when she went on holiday or had days off, she could trust that the books would be alright when she came back, a compliment indeed.

It was here that I met once more the man to whom I wrote asking for a job on the railway, Mr V.H. Jury. Branksome came under his jurisdiction at Bournemouth West and he would come regularly to sign the various books and forms appertaining to the workings. He was a nice old man, getting very near retiring age at that time, I used to look on him with some awe, for was he not in charge of the second most important station on the South Western Division of the

The station building at Branksome in 1963, still with its Southern Railway sign. The station opened in June 1893 with the opening of the Branksome curve.

Southern Railway? It was always said by the hierarchy at Waterloo that if all was well at Bournemouth West then all was well with the South Western Division, and he made sure with an iron hand in a velvet glove that would be the case always.It is so today that if you were a Bournemouth West man then you were somebody. There are but a few left and they still say that 'I was there' and proud of it.

'Passenger' wise, Branksome was not all that industrious, but to me it was a glorified enquiries office, the phone was non-stop with people finding the Bournemouth number to be always engaged. Conversations would commence with, 'I wonder if you can help me, I have been trying to get your office at Bournemouth for ages'. We did our best and I earned my first commendation there from a lady who came to the window to find out how to get to Reading. I had been there only a few days previously and knew the platform at Basingstoke where the Reading train went from and I was able to give her all the relevant information that she would require. The lady on completion of her journey wrote a nice letter to the Stationmaster at Bournemouth West saying that all that I had told her had worked out perfectly, a copy of the letter was sent to me with a footnote, 'well done' in it.

The offices of two Inspectors, Vic Rooke, and Train Inspector who was always known as 'Tiger' Barrett, were

right next door to our office. Those were early days for Vic Rooke, (he had replaced recently retired Inspector Parfitt, I can't remember his forename,) and he was to become a legend in his own time. Each train that stopped at Branksome had to be attended to, platforms, bridge, booking office and booking hall kept clean and tidy, tickets issued and phones answered and the tradition of polishing that brass bell on the outside wall was carried on, only this time I could press the plunger to my heart's content with no fear of reprisal, I did too, just to make sure it still worked.

After a while the services of a booking clerk were dispensed with and a porter was employed for most of the duties other than the office. Gracie Brown, who had by now relinquished her guard's job, (you'll remember I wrote that she was one of the first lady guards at Bournemouth and came from Wimborne,) Grace and Ivy got along like a house on fire, a good combination. On my turn was a very nice young lady, Jessie, about my age, and lived up the road from me. I got to be sweet on Jessie but nothing ever came of it, and I think she married a fireman in the end. A gentleman later to occupy a porter's post, was a Harry Theobald, nearing retirement, and now serving out his time after coming from Bournemouth West where the work was becoming too much for him.

Harry was a charming man in every way, frail looking,

tall with piercing blue eyes, quiet spoken, very knowledgeable. I was able to learn a lot about the railways around Bournemouth West and surrounding areas from him. On reflection, I think that he must have come from the London area at sometime, he had that slight trace of cockney flavour in his talk. I have always thought of him as one of my 'if onlys', if only I had committed to paper or to better memory what he had related to me when we were sat down together, if only I could recall what happened in the days of his youth, I have, over the years, met many people like Harry who 'if only' I had.

Two signalmen completed the staff at Branksome, Reg Cook and Ben Hopkins. Reg gained himself quite a reputation for his insistence on the correct headcode discs being displayed on the engines that arrived outside his signalbox on their way round the triangle. A few of the drivers would remonstrate with him, 'what the hell difference do it make, you know where were going mate' they would shout up at him, it made no difference, the signal did not come off before his order had been heeded. The only time that I had any contact with him was when special notices had to be taken up and then I tried not to be too long in my errand. My old friend, Ron Gingell, was to tell me in later times that Reg Cook had not enjoyed good health for many years which may have accounted for his many unpopular ways that were the hallmark of this unfortunate man. He later left the signalbox and ended his days as a guard, and I know that for his sins he was the victim of many silly little retaliations by some of the drivers. The irony of which was, that if they had carried out the instructions laid down there would have been no need for all the unpleasantness that went on. Ben Hopkins was much different in all his ways to Reg, good humoured, ready always to answer my enquiries on the phone as to how late the trains were running, popular among the enginemen and, it seemed, everything that poor old Reg was not.

A week at Parkstone was preceded by my having to come to grips with a place that I knew very little about, only ever having passed through it, which I suppose was the same really as some of the stations up the line, but this was my locality and I knew nothing of what went on there and with no-one to guide me I had to learn fast. It was here that I met two colleagues with whom I would be associated when attaining the position of Guard at Bournemouth, Alf Goozee, the man I was sent to relieve, and Rex Dykes, in charge of the small goods warehouse.

It was my duty once more to make out the daily stock return and render the finished article to the Stationmaster, Charlie Saunders, for his signature. He looked at it for some time and I began to think, blimey, he's a bit particular is he not, most of them just have a cursory glance, sign it and give it back. 'Alf generally puts a few figures on this side' he said, indicating some blank spaces on one side of it that I had not filled in, 'take it back and stick something in, there's a good chap' he said and away I went. I don't suppose that there was more than a dozen wagons in the yard and, as for knowing when each one would be available, or would be loaded away, I hadn't a clue, but I thought that I had better put down something so I did. 'Ah, that's better' he said on my return to his office, and duly signed it.

It was my experience that these small stations were hives of industry, more railway work went on at them than many of the larger ones, the porters had to be jack of all trades, and soon in trouble if you had not learnt your trade properly. The small yard was one of the most difficult that I had yet come across to shunt, mostly having to have access to the main line to do so. There was a small ground frame with the release lever controlled from the signalbox at Branksome, permission to operate obtained by phone. Often there was a long delay before the release was given and then you would be warned that it could be only for a short time, 'don't be too long about it mate, I got one due off Bournemouth any minute'.

I was shunting the yard one morning using a small siding that was parallel to the down main line, the main line not available at the time, when the front wheel of the engine became derailed. The trouble with shunting in this siding was that the driver had to keep a sharp look out that he did not run into an old engine tender that was used to dispose of the slime and slurry from the engines boilers at Bournemouth and sent to Parkstone, where it was tipped down over the bank there.

The trouble this morning was that I failed to see how close the movement was getting to this tender, the driver was taking notice of my hand signals to keep moving forward and, bang. There was nobody hurt thank goodness, the main line was not obstructed, and another engine came and pulled it back on the rail without the crane being required. I later found out that the driver tried to blame me for that little lot, but he was soon told that the responsibility was his, he should have been looking forward as well as at me.

There was another goods train due in the late afternoon and the shunting of it was made a lot easier by asking the driver on George Jennings little engine from a local pottery if we could use his engine to make a few shunts when he came up during the afternoon. Our request was always granted and it made for the afternoon shunt being made a lot easier. This little engine was a picture, a great credit to its crew and owners, paintwork and brasses shone and the cab immaculate inside, it certainly put a lot of ours to shame.

The parcel office at Parkstone was on the up side and most of the traffic came off down trains, which meant that motor cycles for Bob Fosters had to be pushed across the wooden ramp at the Poole end of the platform, ice cold fish on a Winter's morning had to be unloaded from icy cold fish vans and taken across to the up side on barrows or sack trucks. You may take it that Mr Randall was not one of my favourite traders on a cold and frosty morning when he arrived to collect his boxes of fish. Some of the motor cycles had to go to Weymouth and back occasionally because they would be too heavy to unload on my own, you would get no help from some of the older Guards, their main excuse being that they were of advanced years and the old back's playing up a bit, or I've just had this uniform cleaned and don't want it to get dirty on their oily old motor bikes. Bob Foster's were always pretty good, I used to phone them up and say that a 'big un' was arriving on the next up and they would send somebody down with a trailer and I would get some help to unload.

A lorry driver was employed to deliver to Lower and Upper Parkstone, Penn Hill, Canford Cliffs, Lilliput and Sandbanks. I met the man who picked me up from the road after I had been run down by a lorry while he was delivering in Ashley Road one late afternoon, I was then of early school age, and he remembered the incident very well after all those years.

Sometimes during the day it was rostered that help be given in the Warehouse to the then goods porter, Rex Dykes, to load and unload wagons in the shed, fold the sheets, help to put the doors up on the empty coal wagons or whatever, rope down loads when required, and generally make yourself useful as I saw it. Two very nice young ladies were later employed, one whose name I can recall, (the other I can't,) was Peggy Norgate, the daughter of the ganger at Holton Heath, Percy, and who lived in the crossing house at Keysworth crossing, near Wareham. Peggy had to cycle from there, when on the early turn, and after I left I would occasionally meet her somewhere along the way. I remember her as a nice looking girl, competent and very capable and popular among staff and customers alike. I worked alongside her for a short while when I went there again, a very enjoyable experience for me. Peggy's opposite mate on the other shift, (I wish I could have remembered her name,) she was very nice as well, very pleasant and a good worker, I was also to work with her for a short time. In those days at Parkstone you had to be a Jack or Jill of all trades, physical strength being an asset, if not a requirement, no place for the weak.

I cannot write of any experiences at Poole, the next station down the line, for I never actually worked there. It was the biggest station on the line between Bournemouth and Weymouth and the staff generally covered any vacancy that occurred through sickness or leave, and were always glad of a little bit of overtime to supplement a low wage. I came to know the staff there when my journeys necessitated me either starting or finishing at Poole, and what some characters there were there in those days. The two station foremen on opposite shifts were Jack Young and Tom Elliot, both shunters in the yard before they came on to the platform. Jack was a well built, robust type of man, fond of a pint in keeping with a good many old railwaymen of that era.

This particular vice made them no less efficient in their duties than men of temperance, thought I never came across many of those, but there was a few. Jack's opposite mate, Tom, did not imbibe. They were very different in their approach to many things. You could say that perhaps Jack was a bit noisier than Tom, but he had that sort of voice whereas Tom was quiet spoken, a bit tidier in appearance, but he was after all a lot thinner which, to the detriment of us stouter men, his clothes fitted better. Having stated that, difference mattered not, there was little difference in the way that the station ticked over on the respective shifts.

They were both popular among their own gang of men who were fiercely loyal and would not hear a bad word against either man. As on most stations where I have been, and it still exists today, there is a feeling of being in a different world when you come into the other shift. There is a certain rivalry among railwaymen that their shift is not so good as ours, and I have known men when having to change

shifts, (say on promotion, or the like,) put in applications that when a vacancy exists on their original shift that they be allowed to return. You would be amazed to know what comradeship there is and what criticism of what that other gang goes on at times. I must have been the exception. For the last five years of my service I had to change shifts and expressed a desire on doing so to return as soon as possible, but after a short time among my 'new Colleagues' all thoughts of returning went to the wall and I wouldn't have changed back for the world.

Back to Poole, two signalboxes controlled the trains that passed through, one in High Street was called Poole East, later renamed Poole 'A', and one opposite the marshalling Yard, Poole West, later named Poole 'B' which controlled movements into and out of the Yard, and controlling the points that led to Poole Quay via West Quay Road. A small 'gate box' near the Parkstone end of the station controlled crossing gates in Towngate Street, the box being known as 'Towngate Street box'. It had no control of signals and was advised when to close the gates by a capstan wheel by bell signals received from either box, Poole A or B, for down trains and up trains respectively.

It was a Ministry of Transport long standing order that all trains had to stop at Poole, and it appeared to the local populace that on a Saturday the gates at Towngate Street and the High Street were closed to road traffic and pedestrians more often than they were open, which was probably true. The answer to that only came with the building of the new Towngate Street bridge in more modern times. The three signalmen in the Yard box, as Poole West was known, were Bill Dicks, Fred Thomas and Ron Whiffen, I hope that I have got his first name right, for there was Harry Whiffen, his father, who was a driver at Bournemouth. Bill Dicks was a religious man who was known, when he was the night turn, to refer to the good book which was always open on the desk.

I liked Bill, but he was one to tax your patience when you had to wait for him to answer your call attention bell, which always preceded any train description bells, and I used to say that Bill had got to the part where they were about to cross the Red Sea and I would have to wait until they attained to the other side. Bill would remonstrate with his shunters when, their patience exhausted, they had to ask him to operate a pair of points or a signal, and he was not too quick in responding. They would utter a few choice swear words which were not to Bill's liking.

Two such shunters, Bert Diment and Bobbie Gibbs, liked to wind him up occasionally and this led to the window hastily being closed in their faces. Two of Bill's booking boys who were employed in the box to record all the movements of trains are still on the railway today, Johnny Anderson and Brian Baggs, in actual fact John is the resident signalman there now, Brian followed me to become a Guard at Bournemouth and is now a Train Crew Inspector. Ask them both what Bill Dicks was like and they would both say he had no equal, a good man to work with.

On a Saturday in the 1950s, a relief signalman was brought in to regulate the traffic that passed through Poole, which enabled the resident man to concentrate more easily on his job. It was an easy station for a stationmaster, with all the experience that there was on the station and in the Yard

'B4' Class No. 30093 shunts goods wagons at Poole Quay on 25th August 1954. This little 33-ton engine had been allocated to Bournemouth shed in 1947 following its redundancy from shunting at Southampton Docks, when the USA tanks were employed. Up until September 1952, it was named *St Malo*.   *R. C. Riley*

and signalboxes and I cannot recall ever seeing him whenever I was there. The booking office had a 'chief clerk' who had a booking clerk under him ' the chief clerk was responsible for all monies collected at Hamworthy Junction and Parkstone and sent to Poole each day with a remittance slip, which would be returned in the empty cash bag for use the next day. He also made up the wages of these two stations and sent the wage packets in this same cash bag, mostly on the same train, the 1.01 p.m. from Bournemouth to Weymouth arriving at Hamworthy Junction around 1.30 p.m.

Before handing out the wages it was Mr Brixton's job to make sure that the packets contained the right amount. Some of the staff on the platform at Poole that I can recall were two ladies, one living in Wimborne, Gladys Frampton and Frances, and a young lad, Gerry, once again their surnames escape me. Gerry was a tall lad, always very smart, never heard him swear, a practising member of the local Salvation Army and he played the big drum in their parades through the town.

This was a source of some amusement among the younger element of us, but he was never poked fun of, Gerry was a big lad, even if he was offensive. I came to be very friendly with him. I liked the way that he had with people, always ready to help when he could. It was a sad day when he told me that he was emigrating to Australia, it was all the go in those days, and I presumed that Gerry had caught the fever. I did my best to talk him out of going but he was

determined and away he went. He got a job as a Guard on the railway out there and soon after we learnt that he had been killed in an accident on the railway.

It was all go at Poole, platforms were not unoccupied for very long, the nearby marshalling yard always a hive of industry, lorries in and out of the large goods shed, goods trains could be heard arriving and preparing to depart for twenty four hours of the day. A heavy goods train would be assisted in the rear by a banking engine when ascending Parkstone bank - people living two to three miles away could hear the whistles of the engines as they prepared to start away from the Yard. A cock a doodle doo from the front engine would be answered by the engine on the rear, and then one whistle from the leading engine signalled that he was ready to start, I think then it was up to the rear engine to start pushing before the front one started pulling.

A tramway from the station to Poole Quay was still in use and the only locomotive allowed down there was of the same type that was at Hamworthy Goods, a 'B4' 0-4-0 Adams tank, speed was walking pace, and movements to and from was preceded by a shunter walking in front with red and green flags at the ready. This shunter was held responsible for the safety of the traffic and the train, and frequently had to get vehicles parked in the way along West Quay Road to move before further progress was made. A man from the Permanent Way Department was employed to keep the track in good order, and to help him to carry his tools of trade he had made himself a box on wheels with a couple of handles screwed on the sides.

I filled in the rest of my time in 1946 by relieving at Corfe Castle, Wool, Moreton and half an hour at Dorchester South. My training in railway accountancy stood me in good stead at Corfe Castle, I was there for two weeks while the regulars, Bill Mills and Charlie Saunders had their annual leave. I was on my own and spent most of the time writing out invoices and recording same in the appropriate books on late turn.

The early turn was not too bad, after the early morning influx of commuters and school children it was over to the United Dairies canteen for breakfast, then back to lamps and the stock return by which time, Mr Chappel, the S.M., had put in an appearance. A bit of cleaning, attending to trains as they came, a yarn with the signalman whose box was situated on the end of the down platform and too far away to stay long in case the phone went or somebody came to the window which they often did, even at Corfe Castle. The hill on the down side of the station was a grand place on which to get a view of Poole and Bournemouth and I climbed it a couple of times while I was there, once early in the morning and again just as the sun was setting in the evening, great sights but no camera to hand at the time. I enjoyed being at Corfe Castle was sorry that it was only two weeks.

Not too much to say about Wool and Moreton except to mention their stationmasters, a Mr Bradfield House was at Wool, always known as Brad House, a well built man with a flowing beard, always reminded me of how they looked in days gone by. He looked a bit stern but never was, a man of few words, it could be fair to say that he was another of nature's gentlemen and well thought of by his staff and the people of Wool. In later years I was to work at Wool while his son, Percy, was in the booking office, and we got to know one

another well, a chip off the old block, as they say.

When I went to Moreton I met Albert Jeffries who was now the stationmaster, (Albert was booking clerk at Wimborne when I first went there,) he had two sons, Terry and Gordon, who followed in their father's footsteps, and came on to the railway. Gordon stayed for a few years before seeking a career in the Police Force, I was stopped one early morning in King Street in Wimborne by two policemen and one of them turned out to be Gordon. He was stationed at Witchampton I think for a while, but I learnt of his early death when I picked up a local paper to read one day, which stated that Gordon had suffered ill health for some time, great pity, he was a nice man. Brother Terry I worked with as a Guard at Bournemouth, but he had to retire early after sustaining an injury whilst riding in a brake van on a goods train.

Now what is this half an hour at Dorchester South. You will say 'well it was like this ' I was sent there to take over the duties of Parcel Porter in the place of the resident one, whom I understood to be off sick. On my arrival and walking into the office, the conversation went something like this, "ullo mate, what you 'ere for?, 'to take over from your mate' says I. 'She's coming back this afternoon mate as far as I know but hang on I'll ask the old man (S.M.).' He went out and knocked on the door next to the office and out came Mr Smith, the old man, as we were prone to call our superior, 'she's coming back today son' he said, 'be here about two o'clock,' and she was, making me now unemployed.

I phoned all this information to my staff clerk at Southampton and after a while he decided that I would act as travelling porter on the 2.20 p.m. from Weymouth to Romsey as far as Bournemouth in charge of the front van which was always heavily loaded with parcels and mails and milk churns. I kept the job for the rest of that week and enjoyed doing it, better than being cooped up in a parcel office I thought. I was supposed to return on the 3.20 p.m. from London to Weymouth getting off at Dorchester, but if it ran late then I might get off at Wool or Moreton to enable me to get my train home.

Ivatt tank No. 41320 in the 'up' platform at Wareham ready to shunt into the 'down' bay for working the Swanage branch.

Chapter Five

Promotion

The end of what was known as Reserved Occupation on the Railway came when the war ended, and I now became liable for my spell of National Service, and, after travelling to Southampton for a medical and interview in the Autumn of 1946, it was on December 6th of that year I was commanded to appear before the Commanding Officer of the Oxford and Buckinghamshire Light Infantry at Cowley to commence my National Service. Six weeks of primary training there and I was off to the wilds of Salisbury Plain, Bulford in fact to endure the rigours of that bad Winter of 46/47. What a time that turned out to be, snow up around my knees in places, returning from a 36 hour pass and pushing the bus up a hill outside Amesbury. I soldiered on in that lot, and in June 1947 found myself on the way to Singapore and Malaya.

Many lessons were learnt from my experiences that I wouldn't have otherwise learnt. I had never mixed with the lads from other parts of the country and I found out that apart from their accents they all had the same loves and the same fears as me. Back home readjusting to civvy street it was time to sit down and think about my future. I had thought that my position on the railway was not very secure, after all I was only on the temporary payroll when I left and the railways had been nationalised in the meantime, however, on hearing that I was coming home my father had contacted Mr Brixton at Hamworthy Junction who had said that I would be more than welcome to come back but the only vacancy was for a junior porter, and I would soon be 21 years old in July.

I had corresponded with my wife 'to be' throughout my service and was now on the point of seeking her hand in marriage, which meant that I had to have a steady job once more, with this in mind I was glad to be back at Hamworthy Junction once again. There seemed little prospect of promotion at that time but a very sad accident was to be the turning point of my career.

My old friend in the signalbox, Alfie Compton, had died after an accident while on a motor cycle going home to Wareham. He had remarried after losing his first wife to a mental illness and I wrote to him before leaving Singapore, to stop writing to me as I was coming home and looking forward to seeing him. After about seven months back I was approached by a relief Stationmaster that I had met before I joined up as to what I intended to do, or what I would like to do. What I did not know at that time was that Jack Isaacs who had replaced Alfie had already got another job on the relief, but it would not have been of much consequence to me.

At that time, to hold a lofty position of a Class 3 signalman you first had to serve in boxes of '5' and '4' ratings before ever thinking of applying for a '3' which Hamworthy Junction was. I explained all this to my relief Stationmaster who appeared to be sympathetic but offered very little hope seeing that I was not even a lowest of signalmen yet. A short time later he contacted me again, 'if you are interested,' he

The author in front of Hamworthy Junction signalbox in the late 1990s.

said, 'the powers that be will allow you to apply for the position of signalman at Holton Heath which is a class 4 and your lack of any experience in a class 5 will be overlooked. After serving twelve months at Holton Heath, providing you prove to be suitable, the Hamworthy Junction job will be yours.' How could I fail with that offer? I still don't know to this day how he was able to do for me what he did, but I would never let him down, and after being well taught by a Senior Relief Signalman, Fred Penney, I was ready to be examined in the Rules and Regulations, also the practical working of a signalbox by Inspector Vic Rooke.

To my tutor's credit I passed with flying colours, and in October of 1949 I became a signalman at Holton Heath taking over from Charlie Kitcatt, the resident man, who had suffered a minor stroke and who the companies Doctor had thought would be better in a Ticket Collectors job on the platform at Poole. I never did forget the parting words of Vic Rooke as he left the box, he said, 'always tell me the truth, Michael, my pen will always decide otherwise'.

I enjoyed my stay, not too early in the morning, we came into circuit at around seven o'clock, and went out of circuit at eleven o'clock to enable the signalman to attend to the signal lamps, returning back into circuit at one o'clock. The staff employed at the station were made up of, the Booking Clerk, Freddie Paine, who was a typical old Dorset character and commuted each day from Corfe castle, smoked like a chimney and told jokes, and retained many memories of his younger days. When he retired the Booking Clerk's position went with him and the work transferred to the two porters. Jock Queen was one of these and Johnny Drake the other. As the name suggests Jock was a Scot, a great thinker and wrote many of his thoughts down in poem form, a staunch supporter of his Catholic faith though not one to

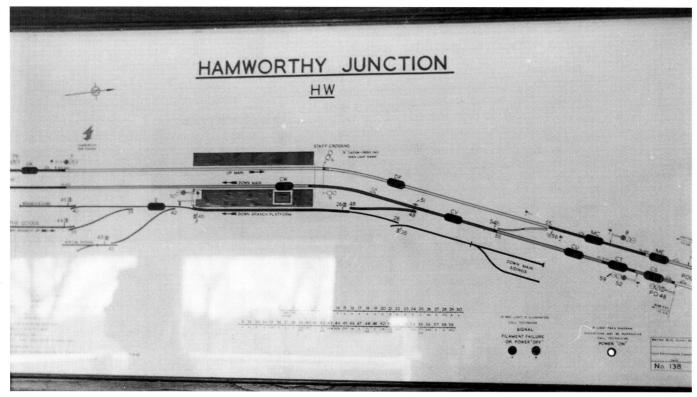

Signalling diagram at Hamworthy Junction as it is today.

inflict his religion on anyone.

It was an experience to be there in the morning when the local Newsagents at Sandford, Mr and Mrs Bushrod, came to collect the papers. Cups of tea were always available and conversation was going on while the papers were being sorted for local delivery, it was made more the lively by the two men being of different political views and airing same at the the same time so that poor Mrs Bushrod hardly ever got a word in. Jock's colleague, Johnny Drake, was a Welshman, small in stature but heaven help someone who upset him. He had a reputation for running a bit late in the mornings and one morning, to enable the Bushrods to get their papers I went to John's house at Keysworth to wake him up. It was also an experience to have to drink the tea that John made, about half a teaspoon of tea went into the pot and the colour of the resultant brew as it came out was likened by me to be the same as something else I had seen! Mostly my excuse for not partaking was, 'no thanks John, I've only just had one,' I didn't dare tell him what I thought of his tea.

I had been there three days when I had to put some of my learning into practice, the 8.04 a.m. train from Dorchester South to Bournemouth was just pulling away from the station when one of the inside big ends on the engine dropped on to the ground, the engine was Lord Nelson class, number 854. Unable to move it now became a total failure blocking the up main line and emergency working would have to be installed for all trains, up and down, to pass on the down line. After hearing of my predicament I was once again to meet the legendary Tommy Reed who was now stationmaster at Wareham and in charge of affairs at Holton

Heath. He came into the box and put me completely at my ease, got everything organised and single line working was instituted between Hamworthy Junction and Wareham. My old mate Ronnie Gingell was given the job of being pilotman.

In the meantime an engine was sent for from Bournemouth to remove the offending engine, or indeed try to, and on its arrival after the working had been set up with the 5.40 a.m. from Waterloo to Weymouth I observed the Motive Power Inspector, Jack Evans, to be on board. I crossed this engine over the crossover road on to the failed train and was very surprised to see a few minutes later that it was being pulled away from the train ready to be placed into the factory sidings and clear of the main line. What had happened was that between them, they had managed to get the big end off the ground and rope it to the side of the frame, movement proceeding at a very slow pace, but it held and the train was able to continue on it's journey with the replacement engine. Single line working was withdrawn by the next up train and normal working resumed inside an hour and a half.

I remember one Saturday night I was booked on so that relaying of the line between Hamworthy Junction and Holton Heath could take place. The procedure was that a permanent way department man was put in the box whilst it was on, and his job was to place a red flag, red lamp, and detonators across the blocked line at our end and to work from any instructions that may be phoned through, for the workings were over a mile away, he was also there as an insurance to see that I did not let anything unauthorised into that section. I got there early, lit the fire, lit my mates red lamp, put the kettle on, and then took his flag and lamp placing them in the required position about a quarter of a mile towards Hamworthy Junction.

Returning from that, I found my mate had arrived and was Bill Stockley from Swanage, his son being a driver at Bournemouth, a good mate of mine in later years. I told Bill what I had done and what I had arranged for him throughout our long vigil together. 'First of all we'll have a nice cup of tea and then you can have yourself fortywinks in the chair,' all went well, I made up the fire in between cat naps, kept us both nice and warm, I could see that Bill was enjoying his siesta in the chair and I took care not to disturb him too much. Daylight came and I awakened him with another cup of tea, and a few minutes later in walked one of his gang and said that it was nearly finished and on his way he had picked up Bill's flag and lamps and brought them back, a short time later a phone message confirmed that engineering works had been completed and Bill should sign my train register to that effect and after that all go home.

On returning to his work on the following Monday, Bill had let it be known that the signalman at Holton Heath, although only a 'nipper' was one of the best that he had ever come across, praise indeed from one of the elders. Eleven months soon went by and I was back learning at Hamworthy Junction box which would take about a month. Then I had a further visit from Inspector Vic Rooke who made sure that the youngest candidate in the locality for a class 3 knew what it was all about, most of my predecessors would have been in their forties or early fifties before they ever got to such a position. The war had taken it's toll and not all the railwaymen that had survived chose to return to their former occupation and the chance for quick promotion came to those that did.

Several old friends followed my trail. Tommy Howell, who came to Wimborne just before I left, as did Dennis Cockburn, John Crane, from Poole who was another of the booking boy breed from there. Tom and John came to Holton Heath when I was in charge and I was able to help them as I had been helped. Tom went on to greater things, following me to Hamworthy Junction and retiring as the Area Inspector at Waterloo after a spell in the many grades of relief signalmen. It was while Tom was learning at Holton Heath that he was involved in a very serious motor cycle accident in Wimborne and was off injured for many weeks before he could resume his studies. Dennis Cockburn worked his way through the grades before being interviewed for the Area Inspector's job at Bournemouth after Fred Barrett, who was Vic Rooke's successor, retired. It was from this interview that Dennis was involved in a car accident on the Wessex Way and died a week or so later from his injuries. Johnny Crane went a long way up the ladder before he decided to leave the railway but never really lost the feeling for it. I met him on trains at various times, 'just out for a ride' he would say. Sadly John was stricken with ill health and his early demise came as a shock to all of us who were associated with him and left the question unanswered as to why he chose to leave the railway in the first place.

I was now about to embark on something that was to give me much job satisfaction. At 22 years old I felt a sense of power, but, if I say so myself, I didn't get bigheaded about it,

I vowed to learn all I could about what made the box tick. The locking fitters, Bert Short and his mate Charlie came from Salisbury to maintain all the works below the levers in the basement, must have been tired at times of me following them around in the dead of night, which was the only time it could be done when there was not much traffic around.

One thing that I did learn was how to free the treadle on the down advanced starting signal when it failed to operate, when the signal was pulled it caused a 'locked' indication to show in the instrument above that particular lever, the train passing over a stretch of rail a few feet past the signal was supposed to drop the treadle back to 'free' but it didn't always happen and so it had to have a little assistance from me in the shape of a hammer kept close by for just such an occasion. and hitting a spot close to this instrument, the treadle would drop. After a time a hole appeared in the woodwork and questions were asked. 'If a thing didn't work then it should have been declared a failure' said the Signal and Telegraph Departments boss. I knew he was right but it saved me a lot of time and bother filling out failure forms.

The following five years or so were to be some of the happiest that I have spent on the railway. My old mate, Peter Bugler, was back from his army service and was now head shunter with Ronnie Gingell as his mate. Another old friend, Duncan Campbell, was a shunter on the opposite shift to Peter and having three turns of duty in the box I was able to work with both gangs. Both Peter and 'Doogle', as Duncan was known, were past masters at working the signalbox and knew exactly what could be done when working out shunting moves, in fact when I was engaged in other things such as having a snack, they both would come up and set up their required routes themselves making me almost redundant.

My opposite mate was Harry Fall who was now not far off from retiring. Somebody had christened him 'Niagara', (after the falls you will understand,) it was always said of Harry that before he came on duty he had made up his mind as to the number of levers that he would operate in the next turn of duty. It took a lot of courage for Peter and Doogle to ask 'Old Niag' as he would be termed, to set up another movement over and above the number that he had allotted for himself, and such a request would mostly be made over the phone a suitable distance away. Yet for all his little idiosyncrasies one could not have a better mate. I had been on duty less than half an hour after relieving him off the early turn of duty when I fell over after slipping on a release button on the frame, and severely spraining my foot, and when Harry was called out so that I could have some medical attention he came straight away.

Another time he came out in the early evening to let me visit my wife in hospital after the birth of our first child, and told me not to hurry back. Yes, he was a good mate was old Niag, and I was to enjoy many a pint in the company of Ron Gingell and him after he retired. We managed to get him to come for a ride to Chepstow in my car one morning, he was never too keen to get very far from home, and Ron told me afterwards that the trip was the chief topic whenever members of his family paid their respects at his home for some time afterwards.

After some time there was a space between trains enough for an engine to run so Arthur asked that they all be tied together. What he didn't realise was that there was a Lord Nelson class engine, a King Arthur class, two more large engines and then this little B4 tank engine somewhere in the middle. Well, this lot in that formation went through to Bournemouth and the driver, I can recall his name to this day, Tom Sibley, said that the little engine was, at one point up Parkstone bank, lifted off the rails by the speed of the others. After that a notice came out that under no circumstances was a B4 to be attached to any other engine except another B4 when travelling 'light'.

I became aware of the fact that some drivers you could rely on to get moving when there was a chance to get them away, (perhaps in front of a passenger train) and there was some that required half a day, so it became my practice to note the various drivers on the trains and the services they worked back so that if there was a limited amount of time to let a train or engine go in front of anything then I knew my drivers. Each morning just before eight a goods train arrived from Evercreech on the Somerset and Dorset, mostly with one of their Class 7s on, a marvellous goods engine, in fact much superior to most of our goods engines on the Southern. It was the habit of either the driver, guard or fireman to ask for some hot water to make the tea, which I was only too glad to give them. After the up Royal Wessex, the 7.34 a.m. from Weymouth had passed they would go tender first with a few wagons to Poole and from there to Templecombe with another train.

On one particular morning the driver came up, a tall, thin, upright man, and in his rich Dorset dialect said, 'yer Mike, does thee think that we can get away in front on thic Wessex?' I thought hard about this request because the 'Royal Wessex' was the one train that you did not even keep the distant signal against, much less think of stopping. Anyway I rang up Arthur James (who else) at Poole and he replied, 'how many has he got?,' I was able to reply 'five mate', 'where's the Wessex then?' he asked, 'right time' I informed him, 'let it come' was his surprising reply, and so I did. After about a couple of minutes I went to replace the crossover points as the 'Wessex' had just left Wareham and looking out saw the goods train running round Holes Bay corner and nearly into Poole. I asked the old driver what his reason was for wanting to get away and he told me that on arrival at Poole the engine was detached from the train and sent to rest for a while on the stopblock while their shunting engine made up his return train, and his mate liked to go out and buy himself a paper - while I fry up me breakfast on the shovel, if we gets in front of thic 'Wessex' gives us more time,' needless to say anytime he wanted away, he went.

Peter Bugler and I were not exactly renowned for our getting up in the mornings but our knowledge of each others jobs saved both out bacon several times. I arrived in all haste one morning at about a quarter to seven instead of the booked time of 4.15 a.m. to find that Peter had opened the box and come into circuit with Poole 'B' and Wareham, and done both our jobs, but he was certainly glad to see me for if I had not turned up how was he going to explain how an 'unauthorised person' came to break into a signalbox, operating same for nearly three hours.

Single line token instrument in the signalbox at Hamworthy Junction, this is for the Hamworthy Goods line.

The early nineteen fifties were the heydays of railways as there ever were and we at Hamworthy Junction were to be a part of them. Twenty four goods trains every twenty four hours either called at, started from or terminated there, a congested yard was the norm, trains had to be found a space before shunting could take place, often having to wait on the Broadstone branch line or in the down loop or Hamworthy Branch for their turn. Weekends we were inundated with empty passenger excursion trains from all over the Midlands and the North that Bournemouth West could not deal with; overtime for any member of the staff to sweep out, put water into the toilets and clean brass handles on all the carriages, some of which had to be seen to be believed.

Ronnie Gingell once pointed out to me wooden centres on some wheels, another time he came across some axle boxes with 'L and Y' on them, old Lancashire and Yorkshire carriages from the pre-grouping days of 1923. How they contrasted with some of the chocolate and cream of the Great Western that occasionally came our way, or the teak of the London and North Eastern, these were some of our favourites. I remember one evening having five engines all waiting to get back to Bournemouth and one by one to create some space I sent them all up to our little engine shed, my colleague at Poole 'B', Arthur James, was kept informed of the situation.

All's well that ended well and sometime later I was able to return the compliment, Peter arrived at a quarter to nine one morning when I saw him come up Carters Avenue and stopped him from reporting late to Mr Martin, our Stationmaster, who came out of his door just as Peter came up the steps from the subway. Again all's well etc., yes, we proved to be a good team if not the best there was, even though I say so myself. I always made sure that good relationships were established with the different departments and I think that I could call on anyone of them in times of need.

I did a silly thing one late morning when I set up a route for an engine to go onto a line from the loop line where it was possible that any movement from the adjoining line would 'run through' No. 37 points with facing point locks, ground signal rods and wires etc., ready to be bent, twisted and everything requiring to be renewed and, or, replaced. I had earlier warned the driver sat with me in the signalbox not to go forward because of this conflicting movement, and later I gave his mate on the engine the hand signal to go forward after a request from the shunter that he could not see the driver of the train that was shunting in the loop line.

The result of my folly was that a set of points had been run through on the Hamworthy branch line, several rods broken or bent, all in a bit of a mess. The Permanent Way ganger, Harry Rose, another Speedway fan, came to my rescue when he said that he could straighten out the bent things after lighting a fire. I asked the signal and telegraph lads at Poole to come over and have a look, explaining what had happened and they arrived a short time later all prepared. In no time at all everything was back to normal and in good working order, and that was about the only incident that happened that Vic Rooke did not get to hear about, or I think he didn't.

Another little accident befell me another morning, when after a lot of shunting about and before setting off to Hamworthy Goods with a train, it was decided by the shunter to take a wagon over to the up sidings to weigh it as instructed on the labels. Having completed the first part the engine now had to return to the head of its train on the Hamworthy branch, which so far I have omitted to tell you

Whittaker apparatus, with the initials of the Midland & Great Northern Joint Railway.

was a single line. Access was by means of a key token obtained from the single line instrument and placed in a lock on levers numbers 31 and 37; not at the same time because 31 led from Poole sidings to the branch, and 37 from the loop to the branch, which meant that a train was able to travel through 37 direct from the main line.

It being of some length someone had a long way to walk back and return for the key token before going to Hamworthy Goods, the whole train having to clear the points before the lever could be replaced, and the key taken out of the lock, which prevented the lever being pulled without the key in. Back to this engine, in the time that it took to travel over to the up side and back again I had overlooked the fact that due to the length of the train the points at my end, number 31, were fouled but ironically the wheels were in such a position to allow the points to be operated which I did and the engine travelling tender first struck one of the wagons side on and lifted it up a few feet off the rails. The driver was a George Barnes and his fireman Donald Barnes, no relation, they fortunately were not hurt, the engine, a Bulleid wartime-built Class Q1, suffered a large hole right on the rear join of the tender and started a flood.

It was decided that there was enough water in the boiler to get home to Bournemouth, which they managed to do despite getting shunted into the sidings at Gas Works Junction. Whenever I saw that engine again, 'coffeepot' No. 33022, I always looked for the weld. Knowing that it was always going to be better to admit the truth, when Vic Rooke came to see me I told him exactly that; one of my old friends, Herbie Cousens, a guard from Dorchester, and an old Hamworthonian, was sitting with me supping tea when it happened, although not distracting me, Vic noted all this and left. About a month later a voice came from one of the carriage windows of a train stopped outside the box, 'that lot the other day, Michael, see it don't happen again' and that was that.

Our old Stationmaster had now retired and bought himself a property in Ashurst near Lyndhurst, to be replaced by a clerk from Bournemouth West, a Mr Walter Martin, promptly christened by another new arrival on the platform, Tom Dominey, as 'Misery' Martin after the Lords day observance man. Wally Martin as he was to be known, was possibly in his early fifties, brought up in the Bournemouth West style, everything had to be committed to paper. He always seemed to be seen with a piece of paper in his hand, unlike Harry Brixton, he was dead keen to get involved in everything. This didn't go down too well with some of the elders and indeed some of the youngsters as well; things had to be done exactly by the book, any deviations could not be tolerated, so that it was that if anything was perhaps a bit 'iffy' then it would have to be done behind his back.

Unauthorised attendance in the signalbox was not to be permitted and I was pleased that his physical strength was not that for pulling levers so he didn't spend a lot of time in my company. For all his sins I got to respect the man, I think that perhaps we were good for each other. I was his first taste of rebellion and he was my first trial of strength in trying to prove that the right way was not always the best way, in the end we just compromised, he was right.

His lady wife was a saint, she attended to injuries that happened to me a couple of times; once when I nearly knocked my right eye out of it's socket when I hit it on a cupboard door, she didn't flinch, just wiped the blood away, bandaged it and sent me to a doctor. He always referred to her as 'Tibby' and they seemed ideally suited, they had no family, worshiped in the Quaker religion but burdened nobody with those views. Wally joined in with many of the social activities that went on, especially the coach trips and seemed to enjoy them.

Soon after returning to the Junction I was to meet another man who was to remain a very good friend until he died aged over eighty, Bert Jellett. Bert was a dab hand at organising, he organised skittle evenings, coach trips, visits to the Pantomime at Christmas time, even claimed responsibility for many of the marriages that took place among the staff saying that 'they met on one of my trips', not the case of everyone but Bert would claim always that it was. He was a colleague of both Ron Gingell and Clarrie King when they were at Bournemouth West and they were all destined to leave around the same time to take up guards jobs.

Though being frowned upon by Mr Martin the box was always the hub of the universe and the centre of operations, the kettle had always to be on the boil ready for my mates to have their sandwiches and in any quiet fifteen minutes a good game of crib would be in progress. Some of the drivers and firemen and Harry Rose, the ganger, would join in, we didn't play for money, just for the enjoyment. Harry had a name for the picture cards, if he held two kings they would be 'Joe Steak and Harry Rideout', Queens were 'bitches', Jacks were 'Knaves', oh yes and fives were 'flycatchers'. We were having a game during Harry's dinner hour one day and in walked his Inspector.

I thought that he might have been in for a rollicking but no, the Inspector sat down next to me for a while and as we finished our game and Harry went on his way this Inspector said to me, 'blimey Mike, I haven't played that for years', 'Would you like a set then' I asked, that was it, he beat me in three games and went away contented for the luck of the devil generally was in my favour and I was reputed not to lose many among the lads at Bournemouth loco, this time the old gentleman had changed seats and forsaken me.

They were busy days but happy days, work tempered by a little pleasure. A pleasure to come to work, in fact, looked forward to coming, it seemed to be a challenge that had to be faced, to overcome adversities that stood in the way of keeping the traffic moving and trying to keep every train to time or near enough. I was very fit, when my mates were engaged in something else and there was a job that needed doing such as a coupling needed to be taken off and a shunt made, or a train that needed to be given the signal to the guard that it was alright to go, then I would leap out of the side window on to the platform and do whatever had to be done. Mr Martin saw me do this one day and remarked to one of my mates that I had the agility of a whippet and forever after that was what I was to be called and even today addressed by some as.

As on most stations there was a young lad who used to come and watch the trains, he turned out to be a relative of one of the Bournemouth drivers, Ted Hill, and I invited him up to the signalbox for a better (and more comfortable) view. A few visits later and Brian was able to operate the levers and instruments almost as well as me. He was an intelligent lad and very keen to gain knowledge of all the workings and soon became proficient in recognising the many different classes of engines that came to Hamworthy Junction. I was quite proud of my young pupil's achievements and knew that in later years he could become an excellent railwayman, but it was not to be, his parents moved away and I learnt that in adult life he had joined the Police Force at Bristol and attained a high position. I was pleased to hear of his progress, frequently imparted to me by Ted Hill and I was thrilled to meet him again, now retired, but sadly our meeting was at Ted's funeral. We spoke together of days long gone in the signalbox at Hamworthy Junction, great memories, we will meet again soon and renew our conversation.

Within these five years that I was signalman there were many changes of staff, Dick Northover came out of the office for a shunter's job, Cyril Wellstead came from Poole to take his job, Jack Hood who joined us just before I went into the Army, (he came from Fullerton,) also came out as a shunter, as did Tom Dominey. Tom was a character and a half, he had a name for everybody. Jack would be known as 'twelve pole' because of his habit of hiding his shunting poles in various places and then forgetting where he had put them thereby requiring a new one every time, apparently Tom went looking one day and found at least twelve poles that Jack had mislaid, hence the name.

One unfortunate choice of name was one that he had christened Bert Jellett, Bert had suffered an accident at Bournemouth West in his younger days resulting in his nose being put out of shape somewhat and Tom, in his 'unwisdom' had called him 'Trunky' and the name stuck, though many of us chose not to use it, in Bert's presence. There seemed to be a different face on the engines every week, firemen came and went, many because of the shift work involved, especially the early turn.

Bill Bishop retired but not before losing his wife out on a shopping trip in Boscombe one afternoon. I talked to her before they caught their train, and she collapsed and died on the way to hospital, and I was in the box when Bill came in to phone the loco foreman at Bournemouth with the news the next morning. George Oliver had also passed away with cancer, the two vacancies being taken by Wilf Selby and Harry Jones, both living in Blandford Road less than half a mile away.

Wilf was a local and another character, he would walk around the engine with an oil can in one hand and a sandwich in the other and was once heard to say that you have to eat a peck of dirt before you would die. He was never married and lived with a mentally retarded brother to whom he had to be father, mother and nursemaid. Harry Jones was a West Country man from Exeter, very likeable man, always very willing to do what was asked of him, he was associated with the legendary Hamworthy outing and did much work in organising everything connected with that. They used to run a pontoon at sixpence a week and the profits from that paid for the outing. Members came from all over the area, most of the loco staff at Bournemouth, many of the guards there were members, employees of Kinson Pottery were allowed to join, all of us lads used to go. There were nearly always two coaches filled and a good time was had by all, and a good many bottles stowed away in the back of the bus

Corfe Mullen diagram and associated block instruments, as in their 'preserved' state.

were consumed, and at the end of the day after calling in a pub on the way home there was not many sober persons staggering off their coach.

A dinner was always provided and you may guess what that did to a belly full of beer later on. Some of the tricks that went on in that bus was amazing, trick glasses that leaked all down you when you raised them to your lips, itchy coo powder placed on the neck of a mate sat in front and imitation dog muck placed on a seat whenever somebody got up. The back wheel was always marked with numbers in chalk and a line drawn on the mudguard and at a tanner a go the one whose number landed up nearest the line won the money. That was stopped in the end by the intervention of a policeman somewhere one day who declared it not to be within the law, though why I never knew.

As I have said the Hamworthy outing was legendary, an institution, started before the war, and now in the nineteen fifties just as popular as ever it was, but with the retirement of it officers as with all things it came to an end. Sadly missed by all the members, gone because there was no-one with the ability to organise such occasions or carry on with the pontoon. I lacked the experience for such a venture in those days. The position of Porter Signalman was soon to disappear, it was what was termed as a 'hybrid' grade

anyway and not generally approved by the Union, and a third signalman's position was introduced.

My old friend, Tommy Howell, had now served his apprenticeship at Holton Heath and followed in my footsteps to the Junction. The hours that the box was open,(it was always closed after the passing of the up mail just after eleven o'clock at night), meant that there was an overlap on the middle turn of duty, and it was decided that when rostered on that turn the first three hours would be spent assisting the shunters. I enjoyed shunting, in the right weather of course, and when on the early turn I would let my older colleague, Harry Fall, come into the box and I would do his shunting, this custom had to be agreed with Mr Martin so that everything was in it's right perspective. If everything was up square around eleven there was time for a cup of tea and a sandwich or cake in Kinson Pottery's canteen and a gentle tease of the two ladies, Mrs Diffey and Mrs Honeybun.

It was around this time that the forty hour week was introduced, and a day off a week was given to balance,known on the railway as a 'rest day'. Having three men in the box it was possible to institute a seven hour, thirty nine minutes day and so a rest day was not required to be given, but it was the introduction of the forty hour week that led to my next job.

Chapter Six

REST DAY RELIEF

I never thought that it might be possible that I should want to leave the Junction then, but things started to turn sour. Wally Martin left to go to Wool and after having a number of relief Stationmasters that position was filled by a man from Kent, a Mr Pay. Good advice from my mother was, if you can't say anything good of anyone then don't say anything bad, and I will abide by that. Suffice to say that I don't think that Mr Pay suffered very good health at times although this will be entirely my own opinion. The friends that had been with me since I came back had mostly all gone to different jobs, Peter and Ron as guards, Harry Fall retired, 'Doogle' was still there and was the 'last of the Mohicans' as I like to say, but the spirit was gone and I felt the urge to move on.

There was a vacancy existing for a rest day relief signalman based at Wimborne and relieving at Wimborne, Uddens Crossing, Ringwood, Verwood and Dorchester South, the sixth day being my own rest day. This was a position that I fancied and after applying through the usual channels, I was granted an interview at Southampton and duly appointed in April 1955. Once again I would be sad to leave a place I had come to to regard as my second home and I love the place for what it was to this day.

However, fresh fields to explore, and the next nine years were to be good to me. Ringwood was a happy place, my two mates in the box were Val Withall and Bill Drew. It amused me somewhat to note that Bill would always sign his name in the train register book W.H.C. Drew, never did ask him what the H.C. stood for. The signalbox at Ringwood would have been an eye opener for the most houseproud of any housewife, the floor

The author records a movement in the Train Register.

always highly polished, windows shining, brasses glistening, and cupboards expertly grained. Bill and Val were super lads to work with, they worked with each other like they were twin brothers and treated me the same.

When I was on the early turn on a Saturday, whoever was on the late turn would come in early at one o'clock and let me get away to football. I was a Boscombe fan in those days and Val supported Southampton, Bill had no feeling for the game. They had a custom of raking out the fire before going off duty on the late turn and then laying it all ready so all that the early turn man had to do was to put a match to it and in no time at all the box was nice and warm. It was a rarity indeed if I had to do a late turn there, but occasionally one or the other had a day off and then I would volunteer to

do the late turn making sure that I got there well before the rostered time. There was a day when I came to regret my actions and it concerned Val.

The carpenters had come to build some new handrails and steps to the box, in addition to that, some work on the line was going on which necessitated a relief signalman being present in the box. His job was that of an overseer, in the absence of the normal interlocking which, due to these works on the line, had been disconnected. He had to make sure that the correct procedure was carried out, a case of two heads being better than one on a situation of that nature.

It was getting on towards the time that Val normally came on duty but I decided that in brushing up I would create a dust while my mate was having his sandwiches, so I left it. When he did arrive Val erupted, the whole equilibrium of the place was upset, bodies everywhere, sawdust and footmarks right across the floor, a sight to upset the balance of a houseproud bachelor which Val was. He immediately threatened to go back home again and to add insult to injury I said that I would walk him there if he so wished which didn't help any. It was, of course, a shock to him to see his beloved showpiece in such a state, but being a nipper I didn't see it that way.

A few days later I was involved in taking a census of the traffic that passed over the crossing outside the box which could have been done from the comforts of the box, but I chose to sit in a mate's car parked opposite. I later regretted this nonsense, because for all his ways he was a man that I truly liked and respected. I followed his example and from then on my boxes were up to a much higher standard of cleanliness than they had been before. I remember one particular morning when it had snowed pretty heavily overnight and I could not ride my motorcycle so I decided to get out my cycle, all went well until I reached the corner of Station road and Christchurch Road, within sight of the box and I fell off. Picking myself up I observed Val with a shovel clearing away the snow from the gates, the box in circuit, fire lit, kettle on and the first goods train from Brockenhurst on the way, all this on his rest day off, at six o'clock on a Winter's morning, however could I fall out with a man like that?

On one Christmas morning with a snow storm overnight, I once again had to take to the bicycle, and this time my journey was interrupted by an escaped bull charging up and down the hill near St Ives. I did not like the look of him very much so I took refuge in one of the side roads until I thought he had gone.

This made me a little late and I was surprised to see a train passing under the bridge as I went over the top. When going on duty, the Booking Clerk, Ken Frampton, went into the box and arranged for the train to be sent on from West Moors and I got there just in time to allow it to go on to Brockenhurst, luck was in my favour, the points at Bournemouth West had frozen up and made the train late. Including Ken, the rest of the staff at Ringwood were the Stationmaster, Mr 'Bill' Bowles, Ted Turner the station jack of all trades, shunters Les Buckingham, John Parrett and Jim Collier. New Street crossing was manned by Bill Harris and Bob White, Les Curtis was the lorry driver and Bill Fosbrook in the small goods warehouse. As in most yards on the Southern Railway in the south and west there was a Silcocks & Thorleys shed. The 'Guvnor' at Ringwood was also responsible for three crossings east of there, known as, 16 Crowe, which was 15 and then 14.

I had good reason to be grateful to Brian Cox at Crowe crossing on a Saturday morning in the Summer when he phoned me to say that the down train was coming, this would enable me to advise New Street Crossing on the bells that it was time to close the gates and, after closing my own gates, could pull the signals in good time and allow the driver to get a good view of the distant signal in the 'off' position and continue his progress at express speed through five sets of crossings in just over a mile. It was my custom after being there a short time to breakfast with the early turn staff in a little tin shed on the west end of the platform after departure of the first goods and up passenger trains when there was an interval of about twenty five minutes. I had an understanding with my opposite at West Moors to set my instrument so that if anything unexpected came he could send it on in my absence. I don't remember anytime when I had to make a mad dash back, the guvnor never making an appearance until half past eight anyway.

Industry was represented by Mr J.R. Wards, the scrap metal firm whose large depot had a line leading into it and wagons of scrap metal sent away by rail. In 1963 many of our locomotives that had become surplus to requirements were sent there to be scrapped and in my opinion were even then much better than some of those still in service, but by that time the day of the diesel had dawned, the Beeching era was well under way and no-one seemed to care anyway. Another firm to take advantage of rail services was Wright Rain, the irrigation specialists, many of their products were despatched from Ringwood Station to destinations all over Great Britain and the Continent.

A Permanent Way gang was also attached to the station, the ganger was Wilfie Moore and the platelayers Laddy Dowding and Fluffy Hecks, they are the ones that I remember. Living in a small cottage close to the line, right opposite to the box was Jack Stockley, a driver at Bournemouth and son of Bill whom I have mentioned previously. Whenever a cup of tea was made in that house one would always be proffered from the window by Sheila, Jack's wife. When Jack was home I used to stand at the window and catch up on the railway gossip of the times in Bournemouth. I had to catch up on it all because except for my once a week jaunt to Dorchester South, I was domiciled on the old road and a little out of touch.

Mr Bowles retired and his place was taken by a Mr Brookes, from whence he came I can't remember, but I know that he was a very jovial type. A caring family man, I would have said more of a commercial man than a traffic man, but not lost in traffic affairs. I used to look forward to him coming to the box and signing the train register, which they should do, most did. Sometimes he would tell me a little joke that he had heard, mostly of the semi-funny variety but I always managed a hearty laugh which I think he appreciated because the next time there was always another one. How to describe him, of medium height, fairly well built, a bubbly sort of man, very nice to work for, I liked him.

Verwood was next on the list, to many folk a sleepy little place in the backwoods, a typical small country station. Well it was out of the way perhaps but certainly not sleepy. It is hard to believe today that sometimes it was not possible to eat the sandwiches that I had brought with me. The staff at Verwood were the Stationmaster Jim Greenfield and two Porter Signalmen, Dennis (surname not remembered once again) and Cliff Deacon. The signalbox was unique in so much as it was able to close out of circuit and still allow trains to run between West Moors and Fordingbridge, stopping at Verwood, all on a single line of railway. This meant that there were two systems of signalling used, the long section staff which was a long metal rod with a brass end and West Moors/Fordingbridge inscribed on it, and could only be used when it was placed in an instrument either end of the section and then taken out again by the accepting signalman at the other end holding in a bell plunger which electrically released the staff for another train to come towards him. To allow the box at Verwood to come back into circuit the long section staff had to be given up by a driver of an up train to the signalman who would now lock it away in a device behind the lever frame, all the signals replaced to danger.

There were two instruments in the box, one for the up road and one for the down and so that there was no mistake with giving a driver the wrong tablet, a square cut was made on the edge of one end and an oval cut on the other end and the right one had to be inserted on to the plate which was pushed in to the instrument and could not be pulled out again until bell signals were exchanged with the box at the opposite end of that particular section. The driver who had given up the long section staff now required one of these tablets before proceeding on to Fordingbridge and so that procedure had to be gone through and Verwood was back in business.

A down train was a bit different due to the fact that they run into a loop at the station and on leaving regained the single line, this allowed a train to be held in this loop to allow an up train to arrive if so required. After obtaining a tablet for a down train, and before operating the signal, you had to walk down to a small tin shed which was the ground frame and pull three levers. One, a release for the other two, next was a facing point lock on the points that trains passed over coming from the other way, and then the points themselves to allow this trailing movement to take place, then back to the box and pull off the signals. After the trains departure this procedure had to be reversed before replacing the tablet for rear section in the instrument.

To prevent the two systems being in use at the same

time there was a lever that had to be operated in the movement set up for long section working which mechanically locked the rest of the frame and could not be replaced until the long section staff had been put away in its box. Sounds a bit complicated but it wasn't really and was as foolproof as any mechanical locking could be.

Passengers for the trains were few and far between, there were a few commuters that went to work on the first down train that left about 08.00 a.m. and returning on the evening one arriving about 05.30 p.m., other than these, summer time attracted a few holiday makers but a sparse service did not encourage people to travel. The month of August brought a daily service to Weymouth and back, starting from Salisbury at 10.00 a.m. and leaving Weymouth sometime around 06.30 p.m. but that was about all. On summer Saturdays a few trains from the West of England and South Wales that could not be found a pathway over the Somerset and Dorset passed through but were not booked to stop, to set down, or pick up passengers.

Exchanging tablets with one of these trains was an art, give with one hand and take with the other; if the fireman missed them the train had to stop and restart. With a fairly steep incline in front and ten or so coaches behind this sometimes proved to be a bit of a problem and some drivers would not stop the train before it had travelled some way up the bank and then it was a long walk back for his mate and a delay for the train.

Once again I make no excuses for mentioning the size

of the place and it surprised me to find out the number of customers that used the railway in making their living. Thornes, the Verwood based timber firm sent away trees which were loaded by a mobile railway loading team, Ted Bowering from Totton and Bill Hazel from Swanage. Ted came from an old Dorset Railway family, his father was a guard at Dorchester who I knew well in my Hamworthy days. 'Young Billy' as we called him was a Welsh lad, small in stature but strong in limb. The trees were off loaded on to the ground close to a stationary hand crane situated half way along the loading road which ran alongside a grass bank, and then loaded on to a long flat wagon with four or five bolsters on the top and chained down. When there was a spare moment I gave help but it was no work for the weak, or the inexperienced come to that. Bill was a very industrious character , never saw him sitting around doing nothing. When he was waiting for trees to come he would be station cleaning or cleaning the brasses in the signal box, he was, I am told, an excellent ballroom dancer away from work, something I was to take up when I became a young stripling of my middle forties.

Another of our good customers was Mr Froud whose business was in Newtown Road, he loaded many wagons of hurdles to all over the country which were brought to the station by his son Percy. I never did meet Froud the Elder but talked to him many times over the 'phone. A wagon for his use had to be taken off the goods train from Milford to Wimborne which arrived daily at around 12.30 p.m. and left

A view looking west at Weymouth. An Ivatt tank, No. 41324, takes a lengthy train of empty stock out of the station towards the storage sidings.

again with the Bournemouth crew that brought the 01.18 p.m. from Bournemouth West arriving at 02.00 p.m. which was taken forward by the Salisbury crew off the goods. If there was under a wagon load to go forward then they would be loaded into a covered wagon labled to some transfer point, perhaps if there were items loaded en route by other stations for London and beyond, then the wagon would be for Nine Elms transfer.

More local items would go to Wimborne or Bournemouth Central transfer. It was possible that Verwood could be the originating station for such transfer wagon if there was an empty wagon on the train, these would have to be shown on the following days stock return as received empty and forwarded, loaded on the same day. Oh yes, I still had to make out a stock return, even at Verwood. If we were unable to get a wagon on any particular day then Percy would have to leave hurdles on the ground until we could and that meant that whoever was there at the time would have to load them on their own. My experience was of trying to load a six foot hurdle into a wagon with a strong wind blowing, if you have never tried it then my advice would be, DON'T, for you could find yourself airborne any minute.

Another customer of ours was a Mr Candler, who sent cartons of yoghurt away by train, if my memory serves me right he had come to Verwood from Rhodesia and set up a business which he called 'Zimbabwe Goat Farm', it was one of the first yoghurt products I had ever encountered and I would never have guessed then how it would catch on but it did, and in the end Mr Candler had to use road transport as rail charges became too expensive. In the Autumn wagons of barley were loaded by a farmer in the Cranborne area to the brewers, Ind Coope, at Burton on Trent. Another farmer sent away bales of wool to someone in Bradford, Yorkshire; some of these bales were very heavy, weighing around seven and a half hundredweight and had to be lifted from the lorry into a box (covered) wagon, one on top of the other, our lads helping the farm workers to do this. You will not need me to tell you who had the aching arms at the end.

The station was always kept as tidy as possible, lighting on the platforms and in the station buildings was by oil lamps right up to the day it closed. The booking office and the signalbox had a tilly which every now and again had to be pumped up to retain pressure enough to give a good light, the rest were small flat lamps with a globe which if the wick was turned up just a fraction too high would blacken with the smoke, too much cleaning of these glass globes would result in it's cracking and needing another one and these were in short supply towards the end and they had to be treated like gold dust. During the drivers strike of 1955 I was going about my chores on the platform when Mr Greenfield asked me what I had to do next, I told him 'not too much, this room and the gents toilet', 'right', he said, 'you finish there and I'll do the toilets and then we will have a game of cribbage for a while', which we did, for there were no trains running on our stretch of line at that time.

I don't recall who won but our few games were very enjoyable, more so because he had not played for a long time and was glad to catch up on how it was played. I wonder how many can say they played cribbage with their stationmaster during working hours, I can. He was soon to leave for another position in Bosham, in Hampshire and from

there to Barnes in the London area from where he retired.

His successor at Verwood was Cecil Tett who came from Eggesford in Devon and was himself a West Country man, married with two children of school age, one boy and a girl, wife Joan took to life in the village as if she had been there for years and joined in everything that was going on. Cecil was a railway man right down to the last button, whether it was operating or commercial he had it to his fingertips. He was a little restricted in somethings by an injury to his feet sustained in an accident in his early days, I don't remember if it was on the railway or not, but he was still fleet of foot when he had to be.

Dennis and Cliff had both left and were replaced by Wally Warr and a younger man, Maurice Cornwell. Wally lived between Verwood and Alderholt and Maurice at Ringwood. I would class Wally as being one of nature's gentlemen, though not always treated kindly, he was a staunch Salvation Army man, quiet disposition, harmed nobody and very nice to work with. His son Geoffrey, later joined the railway for a short period, I knew him at Wimborne as a lorry driver just before it closed, a proper chip off the old block. Another son also came, but like Geoff, only for a short time, father and son being at Brockenhurst at the same time. Wally joined me as a guard at Bournemouth and it was from here that he was going home one day on a small motor cycle when a taxi ran into him and as a result of that he had to have a leg amputated, and was unable to carry out his guard's duties with an artificial leg and so finished his time as a ticket collector on the platform at Bournemouth Central.

Maurice Cornwell was always known as 'Monty', he quickly learned his trade at Verwood. There is one little story that I tell against him. Cecil was with him one day while Maurice was shunting, and said something to which he replied, 'well guvnor, it you can do any better you'd better have a go', 'right' said Cecil, 'give us your pole and go and sign off duty, it won't need two of us will it'. Maurice needless to say, kept his pole and carried on shunting knowing that 'the old man' was quite capable of taking up the challenge. Lesson number one quickly learnt.

Maurice later left and became a signalman at Lymington Junction, on the Sway side of Brockenhurst and it was while he was there that he was involved one afternoon in a horrendous accident at a cross roads in the New Forest and was off work with his injuries for a long period. After recovering from these he went later to a rest day relief signalman's job in boxes between Basingstoke and Woking, and then decided to leave the railway. Sometime later I heard he was back as a shunter in the Bristol area and then one day when on a train at Salisbury somebody tapped me on the shoulder and this was Maurice, now a guards inspector at Bristol Temple Meads. I'm glad he made it.

With Cecil at Verwood it became a good place to be. It was the custom for me to arrive a little early, knock on his door for the station keys and be greeted with a nice cup of tea. One of his gifts, and he had many, was that he was an artist with paints. There were some beautiful pictures of his in the kitchen and some lifelike photographs that he had taken, especially of his younger daughter when she was in the 'Brownies', the apple of her father's eye.

Daggons Road, the next station up came under

Verwood, no signal box but a small siding that could be operated from a ground frame by the key token obtained from the driver, not possible when long section working was in operation. George Vaudin and Ron Tague were the custodians at Daggons Road until Ron came to Verwood to replace Maurice. George was from the Channel Island of Guernsey and fled from there when the Nazis invaded. He had a very intellectual voice, I suppose you might say posh, when answering the phone you could always tell it was George answering by his 'Daggons Road here'.

He drove to work in a old S.S.Jaguar which he left in the station yard for a few chickens to roost in while he was there. I looked in it one day and there was no floor to the back seats. He was a colourful character, I think everyone in the locality knew him , I enjoyed his company for a short while prior to having to go there one day so that he could have a day off. Ron Tague was in the same mould, quiet, very efficient, nice to work with at Verwood. He had been a Japanese prisoner of war at whose hands he had suffered many hardships, but you would never get Ron to speak of them. When in May 1964 Verwood closed Ron was sent to Salisbury in the parcels office and was there until retiring.

Cecil Tett was eventually in charge of the whole line and had to purchase a small motor cycle to carry out his duties. When the line closed, Cecil went first to Wool and then to Halling in Kent and it was while he was there that I went to see him. After lunch he took me to the cement works at the next station down, and I was able to ride on one of their sentinel locomotives. Later we went to Snodland to another cement works to see the locomotives there and I was

able to tell the works foreman that the Avrill Porter engine which he was about to show me in the loco shed was not there, but was stood in the sidings at Sheffield Park, home of the Bluebell Railway. He had to go and look to see that I was right, he had not been told that it was going, but I had seen it a few days previously whilst visiting that railway.

Just up the line from Cecil was another man who was just down the line at West Moors, when Cecil was at Verwood. John Smith, son of the old Dorchester South stationmaster, took up the position at Maidstone. When the rank of 'Area Managers' came into being, many of the local stationmasters jobs were done away with and Cecil's was one of them. He was appointed as an assistant to one of these managers at Chatham. A few months later I learnt that he had retired due to ill health, having suffered a nervous breakdown. I have always wondered why, he wasn't the type to let things get under his skin. Last thing I heard that he had gone to Australia, after recovering.

Next on my roster came Uddens Crossing, not much change from the time I first went to Wimborne. Frank Gadd and Reg Shearing were still there but I was witness to a very sad day when I saw Frank, who was digging in his garden, collapse to the ground after shouting out. The crossing was at that time 'in circuit' so that I had to seek help from a lorry driver coming away from the slaughter house to help me to get him indoors, and ask a lady who was out walking her dog to 'phone for an ambulance. A young girl relative was staying with the Gadds at the time and while Frank was on his way to hospital I was able to comfort them both a little with cups of tea and words of reassurance that he would be

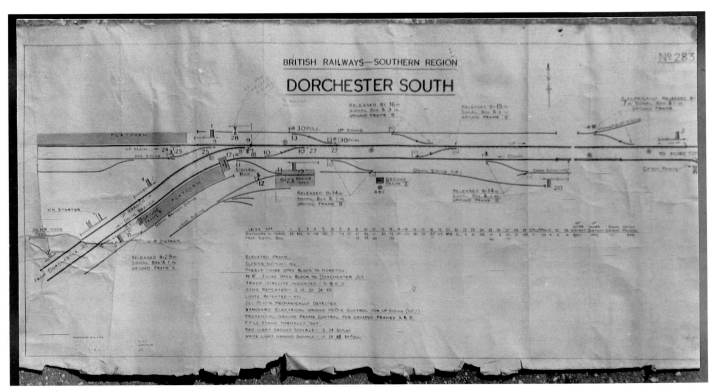

Signalling diagram of Dorchester South, one of the signalboxes operated by the author during 1955.

alright. All in vain when a couple of hours later a policeman came to tell us that Frank had passed away. Reg was shattered when he came on duty and I had to tell him that he he lost his mate, they had been good friends for a long time.

The then leading porter at Wimborne took over Frank's job, Ted Donovan, married to Kathleen. They had a family of four and I was to get to know them and their relatives very well. Ted was quiet, hard working, and after passing out for the job he was always a pleasure to take over from. He liked his cabin to be clean and tidy, signal and gate lamps all highly polished as they always had been.

Memories of Frank bring me to the morning I arrived to find all the lights on, and a cabin full of men which included Frank and Inspector Vic Rooke. All sorts of things went through my mind as I approached on my bicycle, perhaps my clock had been slow and I was late and a train had gone through the gates, I hadn't looked to see if they were still there. I suffered much mental anguish until walking in the door the story came out. The night previous a train had arrived to place some loaded cattle trucks in the siding and Frank had inadvertently replaced the points causing the engine to become derailed and the aftermath was only just being cleared up.

Another great memory is of hearing the full throttle of the dawn chorus whilst sitting quietly one morning. I had never heard anything as beautiful, although only a few yards from the main road it seemed to be well out in the country, a proper haven for all the wildlife, including a nest of adders that I came across in the field opposite.

Next stop, my home town Wimborne, many of my colleagues had associated me with Wimborne box and being resident there, but I wasn't, just one day a week for nine years, as per roster. Things were much changed there the second time around. The girls had all gone, the 'Colonel' was retired, the S.M. was now a Mr Lillington. His leading porter was Don Wareham, shunters were Nobby Hall and Fred Smith, Sammy Upward was still signalman but George Rolls successor was Stan Woodrow who was once at Broadstone. The two booking clerks were Jimmy Howell and Stan Tubbs, chief clerk in the goods office was George Elkins, in charge of the warehouse was Arthur Cooper, who although living locally came to us from Poole.

The Permanent Way Inspector was now based at Bournemouth; the Carriage and Wagon at Poole; the Signal and Telegraph still had a depot here, Joe Lowman was the head man, Dennis Curran and old faithful Ernie Prior his assistants. Mr Lillington was 'George' and many of his staff lived in fear of him. He was one to speak rather loudly at times, something like a Sergeant Major on the parade ground and many of his ways resembled a man of that rank. I learnt to live with him but can't say that I took to him very much, the lesson was never to argue with him for he was never wrong.

I was looking out of the box one morning watching him and Ted Donovan having a go over something and I shouted out that it would be better if he bought himself a little greenhouse and got to working in that instead of upsetting the leading porter. To my utter amazement he just smiled and went back to his office leaving Ted in complete bewilderment as to why my name had not gone onto a 'form one' for my insolence. He came a bit more tolerant after that, he

must have been taken by surprise, but he was still not one to take liberties with, in jest or otherwise. Besides having a sister Ivy at Branksome, he also had a brother who was an S.M. on the Fawley branch and was said to be much different from George.

The signalbox staff underwent changes when Sam Upward retired a few months after I came back in 1955. Bert Scriven, the porter signalman, took over full time and a man from the platform, Bill Norman, took over as Porter Signalman and this is how they were up to the time the line was closed.

The two shunters, Nobby Hall and Fred Smith were quite some characters. Nobby was an ex-army man who had been in India and had something to do with horses and had been injured by one some time or other giving him a slight limp. He was renowned for wearing wellington boots in the summer and plimsolls in the winter. I felt sorry for him in winter time when in all weathers he rode a bicycle from Rossmore to Wimborne sometimes arriving wet through or shrammed solid with the cold. An artful old codger, he would see that the kettle was on when I got there at 3.55 a.m. so that I could make him the tea before we started work. He also had a habit of climbing on to the footplate and helping himself from the tea can. The train crews got to know this and I don't think that half the time he knew what he was drinking, it wasn't always tea.

A story goes that someone gave him some chocolate one day which Nobby gratefully accepted. Being on late turn it was his habit to catch the bus home. It is said that the conductor made him stand on the platform all the way noting the smell and the colour of his shoes being different front from back, a victim of laxative chocolate. When he was nearing retirement the old feller got himself a small auto bike to ride. After the official age for retirement he stopped on for a while doing such jobs as crossing keeper at far away places on the Somerset and Dorset line. After finishing completely he didn't live very long, another of life's characters that will be long remembered.

His opposite mate, Fred Smith arrived in Wimborne as a shunter from Canford crossing. His son George, was a fireman at Bournemouth, both of them lived locally. I was always of the opinion that it was a bit late in life to go shunting but Fred seemed to be a rough and ready type and one that I wouldn't pick an argument with at any cost, even at his age, for he was well into his late fifties by then. We used to have some good natured banter with Fred, threatening to come up and knock my block off if I didn't behave and I never lost the sight of the fact that if he was in any way serious of carrying out his threats I would have to make myself scarce pretty quick. We worked well together and I sometimes had to run down the twenty seven steps of the box to do a little job that would save him a few steps. After retiring age, Fred did the same as Nobby and worked on crossings until he reached the age of seventy when retirement was compulsory. He lived into his eighties and it was my pleasure to meet him often walking in the town, still as spritely as ever.

I also worked with his son, George, he was a driver when I was a guard at Bournemouth. In later years, he went to be a driver in London and lived in Feltham before returning to Bournemouth and Wimborne. His wife Cynthia, was a Wimborne girl, and sad to relate, she came down one morning to find George dead on the floor and he was only just past fifty years of age.

It must have been sometime in 1961 or 62 when George Lillington retired and Mr Henbest came from Uckfield in Sussex and I remember saying that he had possibly jumped from the frying pan into the fire as closure of the line seemed to be in the wind in these days, but he, like the rest of us, refused to believe that such a catastrophe could occur. On May 4th 1964 it did, and with all haste in the world the line between Lymington Junction and Ringwood was taken up, but not before a bizarre accident occurred.

Some wagons that were being loaded by the contractors ran away and landed up in Ringwood Station, striking a parcel train that was at the platform being loaded. On their way down the wagons had passed through three sets of crossings, demolishing a pair of gates at Crowe crossing just before a school bus was due to go over. Mercifully no-one was injured in the escapade. One parcel van was derailed in the station,the guard had heard them coming and shouted a warning so that everyone on the platform was able to get out of the way in time. There was no-one brought to book to explain how it had happened, the men concerned, it is said, had gone away and would not return to the site.

It is all in the past now but it left everybody wondering what would have happened if the parcel train had not been there, for it was nearly ready to go, and the runaways had gone through New Street and Christchurch Road crossings. The line remained open for a goods train and a parcel train to run daily to Ringwood but this didn't last long before it was taken up from Ringwood to West Moors. Allowing trains to run into the Army Petroleum Depot up to the mid 1970s when it was decided that everything would go by road, and that signalled the end of the road for the old road.

When that happened we lost some very promising railwaymen at Wimborne. Nobby Hall and Fred Smith had retired, Jack King and Ron Spragg were now the shunters, (Ron had married Jack's sister), Peter Purchase and Geoff

Warr were the two lorry drivers, a host of young lads had joined hoping for a career on the railway and were very disappointed when they were told that no places could be found for them. Among them were, Peter Stroud, son of Ganger Nan, Michael Allen, Ken Bridle, Tony Mills, 'Whacker' Lewis and two older men, Bill Large and Tony Coyne. Ted Henbest went to Poole as Mr Hurley's second man after May 1964 and was in charge of the line to Wimborne until it finally gave up the ghost.

The last station on my roster was Dorchester South and it was different from the others in that it was the only one on the old Southern Railway main line, and in fact, the last one on that line. The line from there to Weymouth was the property of the old Great Western Railway and we had what was termed as 'running powers' over it in exchange allowing them the running powers as far as Wool, though I never recall them taking advantage of said powers. All the up trains from Weymouth had first to go towards Moreton and then reverse back into the station, controlled by a reversing signal which in the dark would show a purple aspect when in the clear position. This was a throwback to the days when the station was designed for the line to go on to Lyme Regis, but further progress was barred by the G.W.R. building their line from Castle Cary on down to Weymouth. When I first went to Dorchester South to take up duty the Stationmaster was a Mr Walter Channon who had the reputation of being a stickler for discipline, I had been told by Jack Isaacs at Hamworthy Junction, when he knew that I was going there, that there was a man that I would have to watch out for, I wouldn't play him up as I had done some. With this fresh in my mind at the time provoked a challenge, whether it was within me to tame this unknown quantity of a man reputed for standing no nonsense. I need not have worried, he tamed me in the end. Once again, all that was said of him was false, his rule was that of an iron hand in a velvet glove. He had succeeded one of the old brigade of railwaymen, Mr Smith an easy going man who more or less let the station run itself providing nothing went wrong, then all was well. It became the task of Wally Channon to tighten up many things a little, and some of the measures that he took were a trifle unpopular with many members of the staff but it had to be done.Those that remained readily agreed that it was all for the best and were very loyal

My two colleagues in the box were Frank Bascombe and Gerry Matcham. Frank wasn't far off from retiring and I was grateful to him for his help in preparing me for my examination by Vic Rooke, in my knowledge of the local conditions, and in my ability to work the box on

The 07.55 Birmingham - Weymouth service soon after passing Yeovil Pen Mill. No. 4978 *Westwood Hall* is in charge of this train in July 1964 which is about to run down the GWR route through Maiden Newton and Dorchester West. *W. L. Underhay*

my own. Gerry was a man of my own age and replaced an ex Hamworthy man who had returned home after early turn, sat in the chair and passed away. His name was Les Howe, although living in one of the cottages at Hamworthy Junction, he spent many of the war years in a box at Lockerley sidings, a military installation just outside Dunbridge.

Gerry was like me, he liked to mix a little fun with the serious side of our job and in latter times was to cause our Stationmaster more than once to scratch his head and enquire as to who was in the box that day, 'looks like some of Master Matcham's work', he would say, but it wasn't always. The signalbox was situated on the Moreton side at the end of the down platform, high up and at right angles to the track, a good view of the station and the shunting yard on the up side and the down sidings, in fact a good view all round really. The loco shed was almost adjacent which you may have gathered pleased me.I was able to watch the working of the engines and when one of the drivers, Arthur Bishop, took on the foreman's job, he would come up into the box for a cup of tea and a natter, which he certainly could. The close cooperation of signalman and shunter always made for good working and we had four of the best shunters at Dorchester South. The two head shunters on opposite turns were Charlie Bailey and Donald Cross, their mates being David Smith and David James, all very experienced men. Donald Cross made it a practice to come into the box when I was there and do my job for a while when I had my 'fry up' at Breakfast time.

Most of the shunt movements that took place in the down sidings, and there were many, had to be made with the points open on to the main line which were operated by the shunter in the ground frame, his release lever being freed by a release lever in the box and this is where the problems started. Once the release lever had been given then no train could be accepted on the main line from Moreton until both release levers had been replaced and the main line clear. It was frustrating for a shunter trying to get his work squared up and just another minute or two went on to three minutes or so. If his timings were not so good and there was a delay to the down passenger train for which the signalman had to have the answer for it was he in ninety nine cases who took the can because he should have insisted that the line be cleared at such and such a time, and not let your mate, the shunter, do his own thing.

It was during my time at Dorchester South that a little slice of history was removed. I speak of the purple lighted reversing signal, it was replaced by a type of signal used on the ground for shunt movements and affixed to the warehouse wall just below roof level. Can't say that I ever saw one like it before or since. There was one at Wimborne in the Somerset and Dorset days just at the Poole end of the up platform and prior to the station closing. One of the lads found a purple glass in one of the drawers of a cupboard in the room next to the Stationmaster's office. the signal must have been removed at the turn of this century or soon after.

There was a small siding about a quarter of a mile away on the up side and used to stable wagons for Eddisons, the steam roller manufacturers, access was from the main line, and again operated by a release lever from the signalbox. I don's suppose that there were half a dozen times that I saw it used and I was there on the day that it was taken up. The day of the steam roller had come to an end, replaced by diesel engined monstrosities, the machinery required for their building being transported by road. No more need for heavy plant by rail, another siding lost to the modern age. I can look back on my days at Dorchester with a great amount of pleasure, my relations with all the staff was first class. Wally Channon I had grown to like very much, I was to find out that he had a grand sense of humour, was firm, but always very fair and understanding and yes, I did play him up a bit one day.

Jack Burt, a porter on the platform, an ex farmworker, was one of life's characters and I am honoured to think that I was one of his favourites. During a lull in the traffic one morning I wandered on down to see Jack and get some stove blacking to clean the box stove, or so I told him. Little did he know what a foul deed was about to take place! I had observed that our head man would appear just before the up Royal Wessex ran in, adorned in a nice pair of white gloves. I placed a liberal amount of this black stove polish on the underside of his door handle and retired back to the box. My unlawful labours were rewarded when he next appeared on the platform minus white gloves, he approached Jack and said, 'well Burt, I take it that either Master Matcham or Master Webb is up there this morning'. Poor Jack was lost for words when he realised what part his tin of stove polish had been responsible for, and would remember the incident for many years afterwards, chuckling away as he reminded me of it.

Another of my good friends was the booking clerk, Alfie Whitebarrow. Many of the forms that were in use in a signalbox were in his office and I would 'phone him up and ask for some. Sometimes they would appear via one of the platform staff and sometimes when there was an opportunity Alf would bring them up himself, accepting a cup of tea and a review of everything that went on. Another of my Dorset friends was the Permanent Way ganger Len Burden, for some reason always referred to as 'Nigel' Burden. His stretch of track invariably won the best kept track award, his reward for this was promotion to Inspector in his last few years and he made a very good Inspector as well.

I can remember one day when he didn't quite stick to the rules when he was a ganger though. Knowing that I was coming on to do the late turn he waited until I arrived and then asked me if he could take this travelling crane from the middle siding; next to the platform, there were two sidings going back on to a stop block, and used to stable parcels, vans or coaches that might be attached to outgoing passenger trains. Len wanted to take this crane out on to the main line and go as far as Eddisons siding and do some work on the track. I never did get to know why he didn't go about it in the official way and ask for 'track occupation' but he didn't bother and that was that, it was also the S.M.s day off I learnt. I couldn't see a lot of harm in participating in this unruly move and so I agreed that it could take place between the first two trains of the afternoon, forty minutes being the interval of time between them, 'plenty of time' says Len. The first train arrived and left and I gave Len the O.K. to move off. seconds later I was shouting at the top of my voice to stop, which he did, with the raised jib of the crane inches away from power and telephone lines that crossed the line at that point. I thought about it afterwards, what if we had brought all the lot down, unofficial move, and the Governors half day too, it doesn't bear thinking about, but all's well that ended well so they say.

As time went by many changes of staff took place. My two mates in the box left, Frank retired, Gerry went to the Wool box, much nearer home for him. They were replaced by Bill Penny from Stratton, just outside Dorchester, and Reg Dimond from Yeovil; both were signalmen transferring from one station to another. The two head shunters found other occupations; Charlie Bailey went as a guard at Weymouth and Donald Cross went to a foreman's job at Redhill in Surrey. My old friend Les Harris who was with me at Brockenhurst, came home to Dorchester as foreman for his last few years before retiring, his place being taken by Bill Churchill, a former guard at Dorchester. The two under shunters were promoted, Dave Smith and Dave James, becoming head shunters. These changes did not affect the smooth running of the station in any way in the years that followed.

Having two new mates did not affect the domestic arrangements that had gone before, Bill Penny was a football fan, the same as me. He supported Yeovil Town and whenever there was a mid-week evening game on and I was on late turn and Bill was nights, I would tell him to see the game, go home and have supper and then come on to work. When I was on early turn on a Saturday they both would relieve me an hour earlier to let me get away.

Reg was not football inclined but I always made sure that he was away early whenever I had to relieve him on his early turns. They were grand people to work with, nothing was too much trouble for either of them. Bill was the head of a railway family, two sons following in father's footsteps, Michael a shunter at Weymouth and David a driver in London, later to return to his roots in the same capacity at

Weymouth. Reg was a quiet type, very well educated in the local history and I could have listened to him for evermore when he started to relate some of the earlier days of his life on the railway. I only had the pleasure of their company for a short time as they were both close to retiring when they came. To this day I think of them every now and again and of the happy days that once were.

Some of the new faces in the shape of Fred Holmes and Bill Shuttleworth, filled the vacancies. Fred came from the Watercress Line and soon became part of the furniture at Dorchester. A keen member of the Labour Party, he was elected as a councillor and then served two terms as Mayor. He wasn't in the box long before he applied for a relief signalman's position at Weymouth. A few years on he developed problems with his heart which caused him to give up and return to Dorchester South as a Porter on the platform. Fred who would by then be in his middle fifties had also to retire from there and his early demise caused much sadness to all who knew him. Bill Shuttleworth, was something like Reg in his ways, he came to us from Dorchester West. A quiet sort but very good to work with, I think he came from London originally. When Fred left, a younger man, Ian Wallace, took his place; I don't remember where he came from but as with all my previous mates, Ian turned out to be alright and fitted in with the landscape right away and as far as I know at the time of writing this he is still there, the last remaining original 'mohican' of a dying breed.

The locomotive scene was not lost on me, as I have stated before. Engines came and went from the loco shed for most of the day's twenty four hours. A local transfer goods from Dorchester West would propel round to the South with an ex-G.W.R. tank engine on, a variety of engines on the passenger trains that passed through were still very much in evidence. Lord Nelson, King Arthurs and School class engines were among the motive power provided with the Merchant Navy, West Country and Battle of Britain classes. I saw No. 34066 *Spitfire* pass by one morning, a year to the day that it was involved in the Lewisham disaster. If my memory serves me right, it was the 8.30 a.m. from Waterloo to Weymouth.

I also observed on

Stranger in the camp. Gresley 'A4' No. 4498 *Sir Nigel Gresley* pauses at Wareham on its way to Weymouth from Waterloo on 4th June 1967. Inspector Bolland and the driver talks with a member of the staff at Wareham.
E. H. Sawford

another day a Somerset and Dorset class 7 goods engine on a pigeon special returning to the North of England. I hadn't lost touch with the little M7 class either that I encountered on the Wimborne line. There was one every night on a train that arrived in the early evening from Wareham to Dorchester South and returned empty stock to Bournemouth. Whenever the turntable at Weymouth was out of action for any reason the only engine that came our way were the standard tanks that I termed the '80s'. Their numbers would start with 800 something and they were good and proved to be master of their trade, possibly better than the bigger engines when hauling the 'stopping at all stations' trains.

The time arrived on one Saturday night when we had to move out of the old box to a brand new one built on the sight of the old ground frame at the head of the down siding. A few hours later it was in circuit and working order. Vic Rooke was there with four or five others, I was adjudged to be competent in its working, and signed the book. I liked it, all mod cons, easier to operate and close to the shunters, being only a few feet above rail level; no more release levers, all points were now under direct control of the signalman. Whenever I was there it became something like Hamworthy Junction, 'tea up' meant a break for the driver and his mate off the shunting engine, the shunters and for me. I remember in one of the 'breaks' I was in conversation with one of the ex Western Region drivers from Weymouth, Eddie Miller. Being under control of the Southern Region, the boundaries being changed by direction of the government, he was not too happy to be working over Southern metals and did not take too kindly to his enforced transfer. the Great Western and the Southern never did get on too well anyway. Reading railway history will prove my point, and even in my time it was not done to have anything but contempt for that particular company. This would prove to be the correct procedure when they took over the workings of the Somerset and Dorset railway from Bath to Templecombe. There were a couple of places that I knew of where there was direct competition between the two, Dorchester and Winchester. Eddie Miller was not too happy either, with the half minute at stations and wanted to know how a railway could be run like that. I told him that he would now have to abandon the old Western system of 'all day to do it in' attitude and adopt the proper way of running trains. You may imagine for yourself what response that brought forth.

A lot of friendly banter went on over the 'phones as well. I would inform the signalman at Weymouth when one of their engines was returning from shunting duties and say 'another heap of Western rubbish left here for you mate'. The omnibus circuit 'phones allowed anyone who was connected to listen in on conversations, and it wasn't long before I was told that 'another load of Southern old iron on the way up' and someone along the line would say 'and what a heap it is

too'. It was all good fun but as I have said, the rivalry that still existed gave me the chance to 'get one in', and did not go unheeded, ever. It was unfortunate that it was only towards the end of my signalling career that I had the opportunity to meet some of the Western lads in person and what a grand bunch they were, all 'dyed in the wool' Great Western, and so they should have been, more so the drivers than the traffic men. Paddington was the home of their gods and they never failed to let you know it.

Again the old enemy, time, has erased from my memory many names that were once familiar to me. I recall Bill Scard, from just around the corner at the junction, Archie True at Weymouth, Alec Penny, related to Bill, Ben Bolton a Western relief man, later to become the custodian at Bournemouth Central box. I came into contact with many of the old Western guards as well as the drivers. One has remained a good friend of mine to this day, Cyril Crump, still a G.W.R. man although now retired. There are a host of others. I remember some of their christian names and in some cases probably never did know their surnames, but they were all good mates that I remember with a great deal of pleasure and sometimes yearn for the likes of those days all over again. There were many changes of staff on the station in the nine years that I was associated with it; the most changes seemed to be of the station foremen. Les Harris retired, Bill Churchill went as a Guards Inspector at Eastleigh, Jack Perry and Ernie Bagshaw retired, Frank Wilton eventually landed up as an Inspector in the yard at Clapham Junction. Frank Hathaway stayed the longest, being there when I left. The stationmasters underwent many changes as well, Wally Channon went to Bournemouth West, when that closed in 1965 he went next door to Bournemouth Central; Bill Churchill took his place from Swanage and was close to retirement when he came. A Mr Blanchard replaced him but didn't last long, and finally there was Desmond Rawlings, a West Country man who came to us from Walsall and he was still there when I left.

Current day scene at Swanage with preserved 'M7' No. 30053 and David Shepherd's '9F' No. 92203 'on shed'

Chapter Seven

THERE WERE STATIONMASTERS AND STATIONMASTERS

I have written in glowing terms (or otherwise) of the many stationmasters that I have served under, I was always aware that my time at that station was going to be smooth or hard going by whoever was in charge. I accept now that their job in Yesteryear was not all milk and honey that it was sometimes made out to be. The man in the country was a very important member of the community. Many of them were members of local circles, i.e. Rotary, Round Table and

was like to be one of their predecessors out there on a branch line. An old friend of mine said that before the war there used to be some bounders about, second only to God. The war came and changed all that, men were replaced by women and many of the 'elders' had never had ladies to contend with, and many would give as good as they got. The harsh measures of discipline had to go out of the window if he was to keep his staff.

A good shot of the inside at Bournemouth Central station with an 'up' goods being hauled by a Standard Class '4', with another member of the class with a stopping passenger service just arrived from the Southampton direction.

the like. Part of their job entailed canvassing the local traders and farmers to send their products by rail. To keep happy those who were already doing so, and to treat as a valued friend in a close knit society those that chose to travel on our trains. Perhaps sometimes our service had not been as good as it might have been.

I don't think a lot of the 'Whizz Kids' among our young managers today could ever begin to imagine what it

It wasn't until after the war ended and nationalisation came in, that the boundaries of the relief staff were extended. Norman Gould from Eastleigh, Ken Jeffries from Winchester, Brian Maisey from Fareham were to be found places in Verwood, Ringwood, West Moors and Wimborne. We had a good contingent of local men, Ted Chandler, Ben Pond, Harold Ward, Jack Vatcher, Sid Pannell, Ted Hinton, Douglas

Powley, Bob Adams, Ted Drew, Phil Parsons, Leslie Barrett are ones that come to mind. Harold Ward and Jack Vatcher were to become the first of a new breed of 'Area Managers', Harold at Bournemouth and Jack at Weymouth. The old Stationmaster would disappear and in his wake came the Station Manager who would come under the Area Manager but would supervise many more stations. The man at Poole eventually was responsible for all stations to Weymouth, and could be called out to any incidents that concerned the barrier crossings or anything else in his district, suicides and accidents causing deaths were not unknown to him. The estate at Turlin Moor brought trespassers on to the line in spite of it being electrified.

This 'shuffle' caused Des Rawlings at Dorchester to become redundant and he chose to leave in spite of many years service and the railway lost another good servant. One of his daughters suffered from asthma badly and the only way that she would be any better would be a move to the south and this was taken into consideration when he was appointed at Dorchester South. I remember his baptism of fire as is said. He was in the box with me early one afternoon when I had to tell him that his presence was required over at Dorchester West, there had been an accident in Poundberry tunnel and two railway workers had been hit by a train and killed.

I wouldn't be too sure but I think that Des had to deal with at least four more deaths, either suicide or accident, during his short stay. Before he left he was in charge of Weymouth and Wool as well as the two Dorchesters. Harold Ward in his capacity as Area Manager at Bournemouth became a political pawn in the game of closing railways in our area. During his reign at Bournemouth West, Poole to Brockenhurst (via Ringwood), West Moors to Salisbury, Wareham to Swanage, and the Somerset and Dorset were all closed.

Professional railwaymen were bitterly disappointed. There was no-one to stand up to the Bureaucrats in their aim to destroy the railway system. The docks, ferries and hotels had all been sold off, the then Minister of Transport was a 'road man', transferring his interests elsewhere in the firm of Marples whilst he was in the 'chair'. The top men on the railways board were sitting in a good job and not interested in any protests, accepting the decisions as they came, without a murmur. I am still of the opinion today that if oil had not been found in the Purbecks then the line from West of Poole would have been closed, remembering that the original electrification of the main line terminated at Branksome. I suppose that Harold Ward achieved what he had been instructed to do, I can't think that what happened in those traumatic years were of his own doing. After his retirement he was appointed a manager in one of the departments of the Excelsior Coach Company in the old goods yard, in opposition to the railways.

Let's get back to nicer things. Doug Powley, anybody with any time on their hands could write a book about the adventures of this man on his own, a character if there ever was one. In his company it was a laugh a minute if he knew you; if you hadn't come across him before then anything might happen, and did. He rode an old bicycle everywhere, and on arriving at Wimborne one day he persuaded the loading porter to give his old bike a good clean up. Next day

he was assigned the same duty, only this time on a different bike. 'My wife said that you made a marvellous job of mine, could you do the same to hers', said Doug. He was once asked when he was at Swanage where he would be staying in case he was wanted in an emergency, 'I'll be at the Royal Wessex' said Doug. What he omitted to say was that the Royal Wessex was not a local hotel, but two coaches stabled in the sidings and attached to one of the first trains out in the morning, being attached to the Royal Wessex at Wareham to London.

I was in his company one day when he recalled a night in the 'Churchill' at Daggons Road, it was budget day and as usual the price of a pint had been increased. He was prompted to ask one of the locals sat there what his opinion of the latest increase was, and what he was told he would be duty bound to pass on all views that were expressed on this distasteful occurrence. He was told in no uncertain terms what should have happened to the Chancellor of the Exchequer, and during the course of many more conversations on the subject he was supplied with enough liquid refreshment to satisfy his appetite, leaving him no poorer in pocket! It was well known that when relieving at a country station, he was never sent home without a few eggs, a cabbage or a lettuce or a bottle of home made something or other.

Bob Adams was the son of Les Adams, foreman at Brockenhurst and Dorchester, nice sense of humour, one of the lads, but nobody ever took advantage of him, and Bob was very popular wherever he went. Doogle Campbell and I decided to tie the handle of a bucket of water to his door one morning when he was at Hamworthy Junction, knock on the door and then run. The only trouble was that Bob had not answered the knock before we had got back to the box and we saw the door open and Bob get wet feet. 'How could it have been us, here we are up in the box' said we, and though we stood accused he was not certain as to who the culprits were for a long time, until in later years we both owned up.

Ted Hinton, a giant of a man, both in stature and reputation, always a cigarette in his mouth, an excellent commercial man, second to none; that doesn't mean to say that he scored poorly in operating circles, he didn't, he certainly knew when the rules were being bent and he let everybody know that he knew too. I only ever saw him upset once, and that was when he thought that one of his lads was trying it on and he had to tell him to get back on the straight and narrow or else.

By and large all the relief men were good, they were all Mr Scutt's own, whether you be S.Ms., relief signalmen, porters or booking clerks, he knew all your names. Mr Scutt was the Divisional Superintendent at Southampton and it was to him that you went before you were appointed to any position on the relief staff. I was reduced to nigh to tears many years later when as a guard I walked into a compartment to ask a lone gentleman for his ticket and he looked at me and said 'Hullo Webb, how are you?', and this was nearly thirty years since I had last seen him.

I didn't come across any 'bounders' among the resident S.Ms., in fact many of them were looking over their shoulders and wondering how long it would be before they were out of a job in the early sixties. There was some up and coming young men in their ranks. Mr Shepherd at Broadstone and

Mr Brown at Fordingbridge to name two. Mr Henbest, my old S.M. at Wimborne went as assistant to Mr Hurley at Poole, two of the elders and two of the most experienced in the area at the time. It was always 'Mister' Hurley, not Jack as was his name. If I had to choose a 'great' then this would be him, one of nature's gentlemen, kind and considerate and understanding, all his staff at Poole thought the world of him and so did I.

He was an ex Western man surprisingly, from Calne in Wiltshire. I used to pull his leg a little about being a 'Western' man on the Southern and he took this good natured banter all in good part and said that only the 'cream' ever worked on the G.W.R. Towards the end of his service his daughter died leaving two small children and I don't think that there was a man jack amongst us who didn't share a little of his grief at that time. He was to be dealt a very cruel blow when his wife also passed away soon after he retired. I have met him two or three times in recent years and has always said, 'Michael , you can call me Jack now' but I never can, he is still the 'Mister Hurley' that I knew and respected.

There is one man that I must mention who I met when I came out as a guard and that is Ron Westhead, S.M. at Weymouth. Ron came from off the Western at Severn Tunnel Junction, another railwayman who was always looked up to because he knew how to handle men; he could mix with them in their social activities and talk at the same level, at the same time commanding a great deal of respect from all serving under him at Weymouth. Like Des Rawlings, when the Area Managership came in, Ron decided to go. They both had no time for the modern system and once again the railway is a poorer for their leaving. Yes, on reflection, there were stationmasters and stationmasters, some better than others perhaps, most trying to make the best of a bad job, most disillusioned with what was going on. Who could blame them for that, they were brought up the hard way and taught how to run railways, not told by 'college boys' how it should be done. If you were to push me to say who my favourite was throughout the years, I would have to say that there were three, Cecil Tett, Jack Hurley and Bob Adams.

Standard Class '4' No. 76008 arrives at Wimborne in 1963. Note the two lines on the right are full with wagons and carriages. The headcode denotes a train for Bournemouth West.

Chapter Eight

OF CHARACTERS AND KINGS

We had some characters on the railway in my time, one was Jack Riggs, a guard at Hamworthy Junction. I was in his company one afternoon in the porters room while he was waiting for his train to go home to Moreton, from where he commuted each day, when he related the following story to me. Being a Dorset man, born and bred it made it more entertaining for me. 'The missus said to I last wick end that she were off to er sisters for the wick end and off er went. I thought that I ad time to swip thic chimbly till I came to the last un and then I went out the door and looked. No, it wern't poking out over the top as twas sposed to. Funny, wonder were the thing be! So i went in our bedroom, zoot! zoot! thee couldn't see cross thic room vur zoot! And ther were thic brush, on the end of the bed, like a bloody girt big black sunflower. I had to telegraph the missus down to her sister's place in Swanage , and when her got home I had to go to beer vur a fortnight'.

My mate in the box at the Junction, Harry Fall, wasn't past the odd prank. I encountered Percy White, a Poole guard, just arrived with a goods train from Poole when he said to me, 'I think old Fallys going a bit funny up there Mike', 'what's he up to' I said, 'well' said Percy, 'he's up there with Herbie Cousens trying to file down a lump of coal to get it in the stove.' Up I went a little later and told Harry that it was thought that maybe he was on the way to the asylum and told him what Percy had said. I leave you to guess what hilarity that caused among the two old friends. Whenever Herbie Cousens and Harry get together there was something bound to happen; being both locals, they were at one time drinking partners as well.

Talking of drink reminds me of the tale told about Bobbie Gibbs who was at Poole before coming out as a guard, being a shunter there for many years although residing in Hamworthy. After a few pints it was decided that Bobbie, who was in the Red Lion, (always known on the station as 'The Cat',) should dress up in an old white sheet and jump over the graveyard wall alongside and shout, 'Where's my grave, I've lost my grave'. It was also known that the local gravedigger, a gentleman of advanced years always dug his graves at night. On this particular night he was engaged in this occupation when he observed this 'ghost' and ran off down the road in sheer terror. A visit from the local constable next night confirmed that the unfortunate grave-digger had nearly had a heart seizure and the culprits must be brought to book. Needless to say they never were.

Mention Tom Dominey and the name recalls a little ditty that was going about at the time. 'The guard is the man that rides in the van, the van on the back of the train, the pair up the front. 'Now it is here that I dare not go further into this, but Tom could often be heard repeating the phrase, 'the pair up front' as he walked along the platform. He was an ex-serviceman, sergeant in the Army Cadet Force and taught my late brother David, how to play the bugle, which he did so well that Dave always played the last post in the Remembrance service in Poole Park. His names for everybody I have mentioned elsewhere, and those so christened have retained them to this day in many cases. I could listen to him for hours when he got going on some of the things that had happened to him, especially in the army. A family man, he had two daughters who were the light in Tom's eyes, two very nice lookers, as was their mother. His premature demise was the cause of great sadness with his family and all of us who worked alongside him on the railway.

Ron Gingell, one type of man you only meet once in a lifetime, great authority on everything to do with railways, he was the man you went to when there was a problem to be sorted out. If he didn't have the answer then nobody did. Ron was simply unflappable and sometimes immovable. I used to say that a ton of dynamite would never hurry Ron. We became good friends from the day that he arrived in 1944 to his death in 1982. He had suffered arthritis in his hips for many years and had an artificial one fitted, easing his burden a lot. He should have had them both done but preferred to let someone who had been a long time on the waiting list have theirs done, and let his chance slip by. He taught me all about the workings, in my younger days, of the internal combustion engine, valve and two stroke, and it was through him that I was able to undertake many of my own repairs to my motor cycles.

He retired early at 62 years of age, his arthritic joints prevented him from carrying on with his job of travelling shunter on the Poole to Wimborne line after it closed to passenger traffic. It became my pleasure to pick him up each fortnight on a Friday evening in the company of two more old mates, Bert Jellet and Eddie Upshall, and take them to the railway club at Bournemouth. It was there that they could meet old friends and relive their days at Bournemouth West, another old mate would join us, Jack Royston and then another, Bill Cavell.

Jack came from Portsmouth many years before and had been a colleague of mine as a guard, the only trouble was that he had to listen to all that went on in the pre-war days at Bournemouth West while having no knowledge whatsoever of the place. Very often I would be included in the conversation as being there in those far off days, and I had to gently remind them that I was still at school in those days, but it made little difference. In the end I would just agree that 'yes, I remember', but I didn't, how could I? We used to have a day out once a year in my car and have a trip to old railway locations. We attempted to get to Bath Green Park for three years following, succeeding only on the third attempt. The first time we got as far as Templecombe and met many of our former colleagues in the local factories. The second year we got as far as Shepton Mallet, having wined and dined at Westbury en route, meeting many more friends that were known to us at one time or another; and as I said, the third time we made it to Bath.

It was found to be easier for Ron to be pushed round in a wheel chair and the next two or three journeys we made, the chair was in the boot of the car. Ron would refer to the trips as 'The last of the Summer Wine' and this was what they became known as at the railway club. One picture still remains in my mind; that is the three of them in a Bridgwater shopping centre sat on a seat, gulping back a large ice cream like three big kids. I will admit to being there doing the same thing.

Time is always the enemy when things are going along, bringing a lot of happiness in its wake. Jack Royston moved away to Wales to live, Eddie died of a heart attack, having been a victim of heart trouble for many years, that left just Ron, Bert and Bill Cavell. We enjoyed a couple more years or so before Ron was taken from us with a massive heart attack, then Bert had a severe stroke and survived that for two years, not knowing anybody, until he finally passed away and that was the end of the summer wine as we knew it.

In his ways Bill Cavell was another Ron, quiet mannered very well versed in many things, especially the noble art of boxing, which he could talk about for hours. He was another of these immovable types, jogging on in his own time, and an earthquake wouldn't hurry Bill. My own experience of him was if there was an amount of time allowed for a movement then that's how long it took... I remember one Sunday morning while Bill was still at Poole shunting and I was a guard. An empty newspaper van train had to be stabled at Poole for a few hours, my driver, many years previously had a few words with Bill over something or other and couldn't resist a little dig on this particular morning.

As soon as the shunting was over we would return to Bournemouth for breakfast, the sooner the better, but Oh no, Forty five minutes was the booked time and that's how long we took. All we had to do was to uncouple one van and then run round the rest, push them up on to the one we uncoupled and push them all up the siding to await departure later in the morning. To the minute we were on our way, my driver commenting that he doesn't get any better and me thinking that if only he kept his observations to

himself on arrival we'd have been eating breakfast by now.

Another Bill was Bill Perkins, a driver at Weymouth. He would come up from Dorchester with the afternoon goods arriving at Hamworthy Junction just after 5.00 p.m. and then had a break of an hour or so until taking another goods back to Dorchester. It was the practice of Bill and his mate, 'Dinky' Talbot, to come up into the box and have tea. Hilarious would be the word for it. Together we would break in to the strains of the 'Internationale', keep the red flag flying high. He had a good voice did Bill, stuttered like mad when he spoke, which often added spice to the jokes that he told, but he led a chequered life. During the depression years of the 1930s he was laid off for a few years from the railway and supplemented a meagre dole by singing and playing a violin in the streets of Dorchester. He acquired the nickname of Polly Perkins and that was how he was always known, everyone liked Bill, I was one of them.

They had their share of characters at Dorchester. On the loco side, Bill Smith, two sons Peter and Robert at Bournemouth, an idol of mine in my young days. He could handle any engine no matter what it was, big or small, and with Bill on the regulator you could be sure of a fast run. I once observed him running through Hamworthy Junction with a non-stop pushing the regulator over with his foot, which prompted me to ask his permanent mate, Cyril Hollywood, one day if he had ever wished that he had another driver for his mate, Bill always seeming to drive at full throttle. 'The only time that I have to work hard is when he's on holiday and I get someone else' was his reply.

One more Bill, Bill Dodge, not very big but another 'flyer' in more ways than one. One of his sons was working for B.O.A.C. and Bill came to work one day dressed in one of their uniforms, hat and all, looked quite smart. Jack Hands was tall, thin, and talked in a slow and very high pitched voice, a bachelor then, although I think that it was possible that he had been married at one time. He liked to take his time, particularly on goods trains, and was a bit of a pain when there was not much of a pathway between his train and a following passenger train. He could go when he wanted to. I rode on the footplate of a passenger train with him several times in the company of Jack and his mate George Smith, and remember standing on the tender plate going round the curve at Hamworthy Junction one night on a UI class engine at a speed that I thought was a little excessive, especially for Jack at the helm.

Jack Randall and Charlie Richardson, firemen and driver, overalls and boots always shining, they both had the knack of keeping themselves and the footplate spotless. Harry Weller always willing to make that extra shunt when it was required, quietly spoken and when Harry was about you were in for some good natured banter with him and his mate. Sadly he was taken ill at Holton Heath on the evening train from Weymouth to Salisbury and died after being taken off at Wimborne. Jack Isaacs, I have written of him out on a tandem ride in a previous chapter, but you can bet if there was any shinannekins going on at the

A particularly detailed look at Ringwood station in the 1960s. The level crossing in the foreground was for New Street.

A Bulleid 'span can' accelerates out of Poole to negotiate Parkstone bank. The incline here is at 1 in 60 at this point before Parkstone station.

Junction then Isaacs was sure to be behind most of them.

Enjoying a pint in the Junction Hotel opposite with the rest of the lads after the 'London' goods had left at 09.10 p.m. there was a gap of about twenty minutes before the down fast was due off Poole, with the exception of an engine arriving from Poole for the 10.26 p.m. goods from Hamworthy Junction to Eastleigh. This running seriously curtailed Jack's drinking time and so he decided to leave a notice board outside the box and chalked in bold letters 'Take water Evans, back soon', Jack Evans being the driver. Now Jack Evans was a master of the rule book, he was soon to succeed Jack Hookey as loco foreman, and going into the box he left a note which said, 'Unable to carry our Rule 55, no signalman in attendance'. (Rule 55 was where it was the duty of the engineman, fireman or driver to see that when they were detained on a running line that the signalman had taken proper precautions to stop anything from approaching their engine or train while so detained).

The next night the very same happened, Evans arrived to be greeted by the same notice board, only this time when Jack Isaacs arrived back from his refreshment there was a wire along the whole of the frame, entwined between the levers, and a note on the train register book which read, 'No

signalman in attendance, unable to carry out Rule 55, have taken own precautions, J. Evans.'

The railway lost a good man when Jack Isaacs was involved in a missing pair of gloves on a train whilst returning with Ron Westmore, another relief signalman, from a game of football at Fratton Park. Both of them were known to enjoy a few beverages and were probably just a wee bit merry and did not explain satisfactorily to the sergeant of the British Transport Police just what had happened. Jack was found with the gloves on him.

In those days this was a sackable offence and Jack was dismissed from the service. However, Mr Scutt, the divisional superintendent relented and I believe that he was offered his job back and the offence deleted from the records but Jack declined the offer, somewhat swayed by his wife, so I was led to think, and that was that.

Ron Westmore was what I termed our leader. Originally from the Isle of Wight, Ron was the senior relief man in the area, he was passed out for every box from Southampton to Weymouth and relieved the Area Inspector whenever he was away for any reason. A gang of four whose members were Ron Westmore, Dennis Cockburn, Norman Waterman and me, Mike Webb went everywhere together at weekends to wherever the engineering works were taking place and we took part in the electrification of the main line between Micheldever and Bournemouth. In the modification of the layout at Southampton, we were there one weekend from 9 p.m. on the Saturday to 5.30 p.m. on the Sunday evening continuously. We did a lot of work but had a lot of laughs as well.

I remember one night on the track between Eastleigh and Shawford standing next to one of the modern track relayers and remarking to Ron, (after seeing a lot of oil coming from somewhere off one of the engines,) 'blimey Ron, it's a wonder this thing don't catch fire' and within the minute that's just what it did. Another such night between the same points there was a severe frost and no place to keep warm until we came across an engine on a ballast train waiting to go in the section, Ron and I petitioned the driver to let us sit in the back cab to defrost ourselves. I was their driver on most journeys that we undertook but on this particular Sunday morning Ron was driving on our way home. On approaching the big roundabout at Millbrook, went round the wrong way, luckily we didn't meet anyone coming the other way, but the best part was that four cars behind also went round the wrong way in following us.

When the panel boxes came in and did away with the necessity to have so many signal boxes , and the electrification was completed, much of our work was gone, and so the gang of four was no more. Sadly Dennis was involved in a road crash and died a week later, Norman died later from a heart attack after being off work for some time, Ron retired, and left only me.

I suppose that I could say that nearly everybody that I knew on the railway was some sort of a character really in their own way. It was a pleasure to come to work knowing that you were working with the best lads anywhere. They could make me laugh, lift you out of a bad patch, help when help was needed without being asked, loyal to the core. Bad news always travelled the fastest on the railway. Somebody's misfortune in getting derailed for instance, was known down the line almost before it happened and the name of the person involved. I always said that there are those who delight in others misfortunes. Ron Gingell used to say, 'read, learn and inwardly digest and learn from other peoples misdoings', good advice.

In my book there would only be one 'King', P.V.W. Rooke as he used to sign himself, Area Inspector, special class. He had one vice, he hit the bottle too often; having said that, he knew just as much in the state that he sometimes got into, as when he was stone sober. Thinking back, it must have been somewhere in 1943 he came from Salisbury to take over from the retiring Inspector Parfitt and proved to be more than a capable replacement.

People in the top offices in Waterloo had to take notice of what Vic used to say. Whenever any change connected with points and signals had to be made, his word was law. His foresight was amazing, he could tell from glancing at a diagram whether this or that would work or indeed whether it was within the rules. If any of the top brass were not up with the rules and regulations then Vic was not the man to argue with. He would shoot them down in flames and too often did. He would not allow many things to take place in

his area, everything had to be to the book. I went to many of his rules classes at different places to better my knowledge and always said that 'if I could only know a quarter of what that man does then I would be brilliant.'

I was present one evening at one of these rules classes when the local stationmaster made an idiot of himself by not knowing a lot about the setting up of engineering works. Vic just about let him know that it was his job to know these things. The S.M. was quoting things that had been abandoned many moons before and obviously not kept up with the changes. I'll bet he had a visit from Vic shortly afterwards because it was his job to see that even stationmasters know the rules and regulations which this one apparently didn't.

Many years after he retired whenever anything of a serious nature happened the older men would say, 'it wouldn't have happened if Vic had been in charge,' 'he wouldn't have allowed them to do this or that,' (whatever caused the accident), and in nine times out of ten, in my opinion, they would have been right.

Wherever we went there was always time for a pint (or two) at opening time, many an examination of knowledge of signal boxes took place in the pub. The locals must have wondered what was going on. Each one of us accompanying him to any hostelry always made sure that we came out sober so as not to let him down, for he was always one of the lads, but expected you to know your job and work by the rules, and if you didn't then you had to face the consequences. I can never recall anyone on the wrong side of that.

His popularity with all who served under him, plus his knowledge at all times and his ability, commanded respect at all times. There were a few in the head offices that would have liked to have seen him go, he held sway over an empire where they didn't, but his insobriety was always covered up and the chances to dismiss him were very few and far between. I have looked after his interests several times in his company on weekend works and , for what he did for me during my signalbox life, I would have gone to the ends of the earth and back. I wonder what he would have made of it today? Even thinking of going out for a refresher in a pub warrants the sack, and yet in our days the wheels were oiled and ran much better after a couple of jugs, and I never saw a drunk driver or a drunk shunter on the job, they all knew how to handle their beer in those days.

Vic had a son, Alan, who chose to be a clerk on the loco department at Bournemouth Central. He started there somewhere in 1943 or 44 I think. 'Chip off the old block' you ask, no, and never will be. Alan was different from the old man, quiet, very good at his job, good amateur footballer. When the loco shed closed he came over to the traffic side and became a staff clerk and a very popular one too, rosters being his speciality. Much like Dad, he had no equal when it came to sorting them out and keeping everybody happy. It is my pleasure to meet Alan when a football game is on at the Cuthbury but we do tend to talk over old over times and lose track of the game sometimes.

'Dixie' Dean and Bob Goodfellow, though why he always 'Bob' I don't know for I believe his name was Robin, but after knowing him for most of my working life I couldn't be too sure of that. Dixie was always Dixie but was christened Donald. Both were drivers and both were characters of a sort. Dixie's trademark was a pair of bicycle clips which he always wore and a flat cap, the top of which appeared to be covered in oil or grease. Never saw him wear a tie and always seemed to have a wad of cotton wool in his ears. In fact if someone from another depot couldn't recall his name in conversation he would always refer to him as 'that driver with the cotton wool in his ears'. At work he wasn't noted for his appearance but I have seen Dixie outside of working hours dressed like a toff, complete in plus fours.

I looked forward to his presence on one of my trains, his knowledge was second to none. He never carried the faults and failures books that were issued to drivers in case of any breakdowns, he had it all at his fingertips. A train that I was on failed in Branksome platform one morning after leaving Bournemouth West carriage sidings. I walked up to Dixie and asked, 'what's gone wrong now? '. 'Just go back and change the pipes between the units Mike,' he said, I did that and away we went. I travelled many miles in his company and found his conversation very interesting, and his retirement must be filled with a wealth of memories that if someone could sit down with him today and write down all that he had to say it would make very interesting reading. It's a pity that his old flat cap is not exhibited in the National Railway Exhibition though.

Dixies old friend, Bob Goodfellow, was just such a character, much more of an eccentric perhaps, he was never willing to conform to authority in many ways. I recall that one morning Bob came to work in a variety of clothes which included an old army greatcoat and a hat, much resembling the appearance of an old gentleman of the roads. After arriving at Weymouth he decided to leave the station and go for a walk in the town. On his return he was refused admission by the man on the gate despite informing him that he was the driver of the next up train out. The intervention of the British Transport constable on duty who was able to confirm Bob's story saved the day and he was allowed back in.

This incident caused him to appear before his manager and be severely reprimanded as to his future conduct and appearance, and to always wear the uniform that was provided, or else. Well, being Bob, he did just that, and even on the hottest of summers he would be seen in the driving cab wearing every issue including an overcoat, though what he achieved from it I wouldn't know. I once saw him adorned in a top hat that he had acquired from somewhere when he was engaged on shunting duties at Hamworthy Goods, and on another occasion a yellow tin hat acquired, he said, while working in the carriage shed at Bournemouth West.

He lived at West Moors and in the rain would often cycle to work, and in sunshine would drive whatever vehicle he happened to be the owner of at the time. The last one I remember was an old army van in which he would carry his

The crossing and keepers' cottage at Corfe Mullen in recent times. This has all been preserved by the inhabitants.

bicycle and was known to leave the van at work and cycle home. He was once stopped by the police after finishing a late turn on such a journey and asked to explain his presence on the road at that time of night. Satisfied with his explanation they allowed him to continue on his way. The next evening the same two custodians of the law observed Bob walking along with the cycle across his shoulders and enquired as to his problem. 'No problem' says Bob, 'I'm giving the bike a rest, it carried me last night now I'm returning the compliment'.

Infuriating wasn't the word sometimes when Bob was my driver. The train would come to a stand for no apparent reason and on looking out of the window for the reason, he would be seen speaking on the phone to the signalman about something or other close to the line that might be a hazard, a sleeper left in the cess by a departed Permanent Way gang or a light that was out on a stopblock in a siding that he had just passed. These and many other things came under his scrutiny. All very time consuming, but the trouble was that everything that he had cause to report was in a sense valid. I was congratulating myself at having got so far without an unscheduled stop when our train came to a stop at Mortimore platform. Bob had stopped to inform the signalman that there were men in a field close to the railway with guns and that trains passing that way should be cautioned as to their presence. It turned out to be that local farmers were having a shoot.

Many of his reporting incidents seemed trivial at the time but to Bob they were all in the best interests of the railway and safety standards and no-one could argue otherwise. He was among the best of drivers at Bournemouth. They were all good, and I didn't have a moments apprehension about him being the driver of my train, but if it was such that we arrived at our destination on time then it was only that nothing that warranted reporting had come to his notice during that journey.

One more colleague who I will term as a character is Dennis Walsh. Dennis came to us from Guildford, returning to the area where his wife, Sue, had once resided. At that particular time I had just completed five years on the Local Departmental Committee and was not seeking re-election. I think that Dennis was of the opinion that his days on committees were at an end on leaving Guildford and anything now for a quiet life. It was fortunate for him that his exploits in securing the best conditions for his colleagues and his handling some tricky situations while on the L.D.C. had preceded him.

My request that he put up for election was met with a firm refusal, but I managed to persuade him that it was in the best interest of all the guards at Bournemouth that someone with experience be our representative, for many changes in working conditions etc., had been rumoured. Cometh the hour, cometh the man, so the saying goes and so it was. The rumours became reality and after a lot of hassle and many arguments, a satisfactory conclusion was reached when the depot was moved back to the station at Bournemouth.

The bane of his working life was 'whizz kids', these were the young men in local management with no experience of railways other than being trained at the Derby railway college and hastily sent out from that establishment, still in their early twenties, to lord it over men with sometimes over

forty years of service on the railways. Now Dennis took as his guide the old saying 'wisdom comes from experience' and you may imagine his reaction after listening to some youngster in authority threatening that if either this or that was not done or observed then there was always the door to go out through. This was the signal for him to get up from the table and in eyeball to eyeball confrontation with the speaker inform him that he hadn't got a clue in hell what he was talking about, and that he might possibly be better off on the stage at the London Palladium. I imagine that a few, after a meeting with Dennis attending, wished they hadn't.

Away from all that he was a different character altogether. When he was appointed as a senior conductor with Inter City he could walk into the staff room at Reading, occupied mainly by train crews from all over the Western Region, London, Birmingham and Bournemouth, and strike up a conversation in that sergeant major voice of his, causing everyone in the room to sit up and take notice whether they wanted to or not. He was a past master at laying everything that he said on the line, so that there had to be a response, be the subject railways, politics or even religion. I have been there when there has been a darn good argument going on, or the room in hilarious laughter after hearing one of Dennis's jokes or a past experience. Any reference to his wife would be, 'Sue said this' or 'Sue did that'. I met her several times after and concluded that she was a very nice lady, a proper soulmate for him.

His one weakness was books, of most subjects under the sun. I think that Sue was of the opinion that he possibly had more books at home than could be housed, and it was a standing joke among us elders at the depot that some purchases had to be kept secret and taken to the garden shed for perusal. There were a good many of his colleagues sorely missed him when he retired at Christmas time in 1992 and I for one wished that he would put in an appearance at some of the functions that are held, but he chose not to and that's a great pity, they don't come like him anymore.

My old mate Brian Baggs, B.B., shall have the honour of being my last 'character'. Brian was a lot younger than I but old enough to be one of the few remaining ex Bournemouth West men still among us. He was employed as a messenger boy in those far off days when such a grade was still required. The first contact that I had with him was when he was transferred to Poole 'B' signalbox to be their booking boy. His job being to record on the train register sheet the time of all bell signals sent and received, the arrivals and departure times of all trains using the station and goods yard, and helping with the general cleaning of the signalbox. It was inevitable that he would soon be as competent at working the signalbox as his seniors, and so it was that not too much time elapsed before he was on his way to Broadstone and in charge of that signalbox.

I was at that time relieving the vacancy at Corfe Mullen, the next section up the line and you can imagine the conversations that went on over the omnibus circuit telephones. Everybody down the line that so inclined to listen could hear our conversations and often added a good natured quip or two, especially about Southern (railway) men coming over to the S & D to find out how a real railway is run, etc. In the death throws of that line, traffic being sparse, Brian and I decided one evening that we would pay a

Standard No. 77014 at Blandford Forum on 16th October 1966 with the 'Dorset & Hants Railtour'.   *R. E. Ruffell*

call on Bert Scammell, our colleague at Blandford and we arranged that after departure of the penultimate train of the evening I would come to Broadstone and pick up Brian and make our way to Blandford, which we did.

Bert had the shock of his life to see us two arrive on his doorstep but was delighted all the same for he had never met Brian, only hearing his voice over the 'phone. All too soon it was time to wend our way back to our respective boxes, leaving just about the right amount of time to do so, but we had not allowed for one thing, the state of the roads. Since our arrival at Blandford there had been a hard frost and the state of the roads was such, that our progress along them would be much impeded, satisfying the need for our safety. However, all's well that ends well.

After a somewhat hairy drive down over the hill to Broadstone, and then back up I managed to get a token from the machine, courtesy of Brian at Broadstone, and allow the last train in (which by now was close to Corfe Mullen) to complete it's journey to Bournemouth. A little too close for comfort. I am glad that Brian was able to meet Bert for after the closure of the line, and enjoying a short retirement, Bert was helping to tidy up his local churchyard when he collapsed and died from a heart attack, as did his brother before him.

After the closure I was sent to relieve at Pokesdown,

staying as a mate of Alec Carter, for about four months and on leaving my replacement was Brian. In April 1969 I was appointed as a guard at Bournemouth Central and who should join me there after a short time, You've guessed it, Brian Baggs and on the same side of the shift as well. Fate decreed that he would be on the turn that I would be on the following week and it became my custom to enquire of him the pitfalls,if any, of that particular turn.

This much delighted Brian who announced to one and all that he was now minder to the old man (me) and that it was his job to 'put me right' for the following week. Unusual among railwaymen Brian held Conservative views and was noted for his sometimes heated arguments in defence of that party from which he gained a reputation of being somewhat fiery. I was always aware that it was as well to be on the right side of him. I had also noted that he didn't suffer 'mickey taking' from his youngers very well.

I recall that he got rather sunburnt while out in a friends boat one day which left his features resembling a patchwork quilt and you can imagine what bantering went on as a result of that. I have enjoyed his company at work and on the few social occasions that we were together, maybe there will be more, I hope so.

Chapter Nine

BEECHING AND THE AFTERMATH

I can look back on the beginning of the 1960s and say that they were indeed the dark days, it seemed that the end of the world was nigh. The rumours were rife this line was to be closed, and that line was under threat. There seemed no end to what might happen, morale was at its lowest ebb, nothing was certain anymore. 'They won't close our line down' was said everywhere, but no-one was entirely convinced of that, and so it came to 1963. No more rumours now, it was decreed that the old road would go, (the line from Poole to Brockenhurst), the line from West Moors to Salisbury, and the entire Somerset and Dorset line from Bath to Broadstone. Protests were held up and down the counties, letters to the local and national press were sent, meetings with the local M.P. were arranged, the help of the Transport Users Consultative Committee was sought, but to no avail. Right up to the eleventh hour in 1964 meetings were still being held to forestall the closure, but I had got to learn of a lady in Ringwood being sent a letter about accommodation for workers by the company in Scunthorpe given the contract to take up the line, this being in the December of 1963. I thought then that a contract could not have been drawn up without the owners that be, knowing about it. It takes time for these things to happen and to have to cancel costs a lot of money. Of course they knew it was going to close, all these meetings were a sham, a case of fooling all the people all the

time, only we couldn't see it that way then. Money had been spent on strengthening bridges at Ringwood a short time before, but in the future our Area Manager, Mr Ward, admitted that the line was closed to pay for electrification of the line between Brockenhurst and Bournemouth. All the answers to all the questions asked at the meetings were absolute bull. Number one priority was to close the railways and build the roads. Where have all the buses gone that we were promised would replace the train service? Some ran for a month or so and then were withdrawn, which anyone with half an eye could see happening. I forecast that the roads would be clogged up with the increased traffic, and I was proved to be right.

My neighbour took nearly an hour to get to Poole Hospital by ambulance from Wimborne one morning at 8 a.m. Just after I got my guard's job, I left home one morning at 8.15 a.m. hoping to get to the carriage sidings at Bournemouth West at 9 a.m. and at 8.55 a.m. I was still at the Wallisdown crossroads. Stop, start, from Longham, side by side from Bear Cross to the Mountbatten Arms, and then one long queue to the crossroads before turning off down Alder Road and walking in from Branksome station. If ever there was a rostered start around 8.30 a.m. to 9 a.m. I tried to change with my colleagues for a much earlier turn. Failing that, I would have to leave home at 7.30 a.m. to make sure of

The end is nigh for Dorset's branch lines. Here, a special was run to Bridport called 'The Dorset Belle' which ran on 27th February 1966. In the event the line to Bridport lasted into the 1970s.

Above: One branch line that did close in the 1960s, was the Lyme Regis Branch. It closed in 1965. Spanning two counties (Devon and Dorset) this little line saw many varied locomotives over the years. Here Ivatt Class 2 No. 41291 halts at Combpyne on 10th March 1965 with the 12.10 from Axminster. *Below:* The same Ivatt has just crossed over Cannington viaduct with the 12.40 from Lyme Regis.   *W. L. Underhay*

Perhaps the most famous line in Dorset to close was the Somerset & Dorset line. This old sign from Stourpaine and Durweston Halt still survives.

getting there on time. In the last local elections for the Dorset council a Liberal Democrat came round and listened to my plea for a rapid transport system to be thought about between Wimborne to Poole and Wimborne to Bournemouth, to ease the strain on overcrowded roads and ill tempered drivers trying to get to work. I came away with the opinion that she thought I was a bit funny.

Hope sprang eternal when the Labour Party got back into power in October 1964, it would still be possible to reopen most of the closed railways, we thought, as the Somerset and Dorset lines had not yet closed, they surely won't be closed now, was the general opinion. Now I am not leaning towards any particular party, but I always thought that the Labour Party favoured railways more than the Tories did, but 'Oh' how wrong I was to be. Barbara Castle became Minister of Transport and it turned out that she was in same frame of mind towards us as had been her predecessor, Mr Marples, and closed just as many miles of track as he had done, if not more. No reprieve for the S&D, no reopening of anywhere, beaten and betrayed by those we thought were our friends.

I had been posted over to the old Somerset and Dorset to work and I passed out for Corfe Mullen, Bailey Gate and Blandford boxes. It had the reputation of being a family line, with omnibus circuit 'phones in operation, it was always possible to hear what the other man was saying and to chip in your five eggs, which was very often done. It was as though you knew everybody along the line but never ever met them personally.

Good natured banter went on when information was passed on that a large pouch for the single line tablet was required on the next one, the engine not fitted with a catcher. If it was fitted then a much smaller pouch would be attached to the 'Whittaker' apparatus outside of the boxes and the train would catch it on a similar 'catcher' attached to the side of the engine at normal speed, instead of having to slow right down when exchanged by hand. The old enemy, the G.W.R. or the Western Region as they were then, were allowed to take over the line from Bath to Templecombe and this signed the death warrant of the whole of the old Somerset and Dorset. It was almost unbelievable to see trains out of

Templecombe going away to Bath just as the train from Bournemouth was running in, the next one perhaps in three hours time.

Traffic that once passed over the line was diverted many extra miles over Western metals that was destined for the southern end. One train from Avonmouth went via Bath, Westbury, Salisbury, Southampton and Bournemouth to Blandford, officialdom gone absolutely stark raving bonkers. The long standing 'Pines Express' was re-routed via Reading, and no further trains from the North or the Midlands ever came our way again. The line was reduced to that of a backwater branch line and the track, bridges and stations allowed to deteriorate so that so many speed restrictions applied keeping any sort of timetable was out of the question which made it inevitable that it would die of sheer frustration and that's eventually what happened.

I know that I have been accused of sentimentality many times over the years when relating to closure of railways, especially of the S & D, but I always say this 'when next you are out for a ride or going on holiday and are stuck outside Bath for what seems like hours trying to get into, or through, just think of what might have taken place if there was still a railway there'. It possibly could have been turned into some sort of transit system that may have relieved some of the congestion on the roads that exists in Bath today. A couple of years ago coming back off holiday it took me 65 minutes from the top of the hill at Lansdown to the traffic lights at the bottom, and nearly as long on the previous Sunday trying to get into the city from the other way. Look at the situation in other places where the lines have disappeared, the same problems are there too. Not much good looking at the railways for some sort of solution, there ain't one and they will never build another one, though you may move the blockage along a bit if you build another road. It's a thought you know!

What follows now is something that I once said that I would never write about, and when asked why I said that, I would be hypocritical of many things that went on. When I thought about it I realised that it occupied the last 24 years of my life on the railway and I couldn't leave it at that could I? After the end of the S & D, I went to Pokesdown for nearly four months on 12 hours all the time, six hours at home and then back to work. Sundays meant that I finished at six in the morning , on again at two until ten, and then back on early turn on the Monday morning. When I complained to my Area Manager, Mr Ward about it he was most put out. I must have been the first one to complain about earning good money or that was the impression I got. Soon after that I got a move and it was back to relief work in my own area, Hamworthy Junction, Worgret Junction, Wool, Moreton and Dorchester South, which brings me to one evening in the box at Hamworthy Junction when the 'phone rang. On the other end a voice said 'there's an exhausted vacancy for a guards job at Bournemouth Central, put in for it'. An exhausted vacancy is one that there had been no applications for although advertised on the vacancy list. I knew not the voice then, nor do I know who it was to this day, but I filled out a form and was accepted. This surprised me for I was not in the same line of promotion in those days and it was very difficult to change channels, so as to protect these lines of

'West Country' Class Pacifics, Nos. 34006 *Bude* and 34057 *Biggin Hill*, are seen near Evercreech Junction on the last day of passenger operation on the Somerset and Dorset line on 5th March 1966.
John H. Bird

promotion in other grades. No protests as far as I know were received from lower grades. If there was I didn't hear about them or encounter any animosity after.

In April 1969 I commenced training as a guard, ten weeks in all. The rules and regulations had to be learnt, and a written test set by the examiners to be passed. I received 99 points out of 100, (if I hadn't, then being a signalman I should have done). Six weeks out on the trains familiarising myself with the roads that I would work over, and then a day and a half with the Guards Inspector whom I knew well, Ernie Newham. He put me through the lot, written, oral, and practical in that day and a half, no favours shown, and I was glad to get away from his office in the end.

Bournemouth Central was a two link depot, the senior men only doing passenger train work, the rest mostly on goods trains with a passenger train thrown in now and again for good measure. In the Summer goods work wasn't too bad but in the height of Winter it was a very cold one, walking round the various yards in the dead of night, examining wagons on your train making sure that they were safe to travel. Where roped or sheeted that these were secure, and then on to the brake van at the rear of the train, rake out the old fire, lay and light another one with the wood that you had brought from home, get coal from somewhere (and that sometimes meant walking a half mile or so to where it may

be stored). Not every yard had a store of coal so you had to go looking between the rails for some that had come out of a wagon while being shunted. Three tail lamps were required to be alight even in daylight where the train passed through a tunnel, and there was not always three in a van and then you had to go looking, perhaps 'borrowing' one from another brake van nearby.

Having achieved all that it was now time to go to the front of the train and inform the driver of the load. A special form had to be made out for this purpose with the details of the number of wagons, the total weight, the brake force available. That depended on the number of wagons that were vacuum fitted, and the speed the train was allowed to travel at. That again depended on the load or the wheelbase of any wagon. It generally worked out around 45 miles per hour which to some of our drivers meant not under 60 m.p.h. Some , it was impossible to sit down in, the sell by date for maintenance on most were light years behind. I often wondered if the one I was riding in had any bearings left in the axles.

The trains were mostly hauled by 33 diesel electric locos but every now and again you would encounter one of the H.B. class of loco on the front. These were originally all electric locos employed on the South Eastern side of the Southern Region but on being transferred to the South

Western side a small diesel engine had been added to work in the yards and over lines that were not electrified. They were totally unsuited to goods work, 85 tons of lethal loco that would develop a thousand amps at the first position of the controller, and snatching at the train as it started. Unless you were wary it could throw you from one end of the van to the other.

I always kept my handbrake fairly hard on until we were on our way. Twice I was hurt in a brake van and twice it was only travelling at less than walking pace with a H.B. on the front; it would bring a train to an immediate stand at that speed, and unless you knew that it was coming to a stand at any particular time it was always best to sit down and hang on tight. Good braking with a loose coupled goods train was not one of their assets. Once I found myself on the floor at the other end of the van from where I had been standing on arrival in the shunting yard at Bevois Park and once on arrival in Bournemouth Central yard, both times when the train was almost at a standstill. The H.B. was not very much liked by the majority of drivers that I talked to, it seemed to have a mind of it's own.

A permanent working on the 12.28 empty newspaper vans from Poole to Clapham Junction, was one of our jobs, and if the right driver was on, it was the practice to ride in the cab with him. Nine vans was the permitted load up Parkstone bank which we had to ascend using only the diesel engine until reaching the live rail at Branksome, speed under 10 m.p.h. in places especially after Parkstone station, sometimes having to stop because the booster had failed and then having to start on the gradient. The train was on an Eastleigh diagram and was the last train that they worked off on early turn before being relieved at Eastleigh with another Eastleigh driver. I got to know many of them really well, some having been at Bournemouth as a fireman before going to Eastleigh to get their jobs as drivers. Many returned home whenever there was a vacancy in later years, having commuted from Bournemouth to Eastleigh at all times of the day and night for many years. One of my good friends, Barry Jeans who was away for seventeen years, before his turn to come home, was one of those.

Working parcels trains was one of my favourite pastimes, but it was one Saturday morning whilst in the cab of a 33 class loco with an old friend off the S & D, Steve Penny, that I was to witness the suicide of a young woman at the entrance to Bincombe tunnel. We had worked this parcel train from Bournemouth stopping at Poole, Wareham, Dorchester and were on our way to Weymouth after Steve had helped me unload the vans so that we would have more time for our snack before we had to work the 7.34 'Royal Wessex' to Waterloo. We were approaching the mouth of the tunnel at about 60 m.p.h. when I noticed this girl walking in the cess with her back towards us. My immediate thoughts were that she was possibly walking the line instead of the road and jokingly said to Steve that perhaps she might want a lift. I had no sooner said that when she suddenly turned side on to us and threw herself under our wheels. It was quite a shock at the time and when we got round to stopping we were nearly at the other end of the tunnel.

We decided to stop and inform the signalman at the signal approaching Weymouth but unfortunately a boat train from Weymouth Quay to Waterloo passed us on the up road

and came across her, head on one side of the rail and body on the other. We both had to attend the inquest at Weymouth a short time later to give evidence as to what we had seen and what we had done. This incident upset my system for a long time. The girl was only 38 years old and was suffering withdrawal symptoms from a drug she had been taking. I vowed never again to see anything like that if I could help it, and I informed my immediate superiors that if anything happened like it again I would never go back if I thought that anyone so involved was in pieces.

I had to steel myself one morning when working a stopping train from Waterloo and on arrival at Christchurch 'home' signal, which was at red, I got on the phone at the signal. Dennis Cockburn, who was the signalman, told me that he thought that there had been somebody hit by the up cross country, the engine of which stood on the river bridge, minus driver. Rather than being held for a long time I asked if it was alright if we went into Christchurch station at a much reduced speed, this being granted a few minutes later, my driver was again an Eastleigh man. The scene that greeted us soon after moving was horrible, bits of body everywhere, the main torso covered by black plastic bags in the middle of the up road. I will not describe what I saw, it was too gruesome and the terrible part about it was that the victim was the son of one of my mates, a guard at Bournemouth who found out a few days later. His son not always returning home for days on end, one of our British Transport Police friends at Bournemouth station had to tell him that the remains were that of his son. I had worked with the boy when he was a shunter at Poole and he had often come into the railway club when I was in there. A verdict of suicide was again recorded and I remember thinking that I hope that this type of thing doesn't happen very often or I'm going to pack the job in. Only one more occurred, and then I was to see a young lad in the middle of the up slow line at Clapham Junction killed by either jumping out of or falling from a train, never did hear of what happened. I count myself fortunate because two of my driver mates had been involved in five suicides and still retained their sanity. I don't think that my nerves would have stood anymore.

The most dreaded word for me on a train was 'fire'. I was working a cross country train one afternoon, before Inter City took them over, when the buffet steward came to my van and said that there was a small fire started near the front guards van. In those days a train was not fitted with fire extinguishers that could be used on electrical fires, only the large red water type was available and so I had to find one of those at the end of the nearest carriage. The first one that I picked up didn't work, so on to the next one which fortunately did. On arriving at the scene I found that the asbestos covering behind the electric heater in the guards compartment had worn away and the wooden bulkhead between that and the passenger accommodation was well alight. I managed to quell the flames and stopped the train at Eastleigh to further examine for damage to the floor and outside surrounds; they proved to be alright so on we went.

There are strict rules that apply to any fires on trains and where they should not be stopped in any emergency. Tunnels, viaducts, fuel installations, stations and anywhere passenger evacuation might be difficult, and these are some of the things that you have to bear in mind whenever a fire

'West Country' Class No. 34021 *Dartmoor* hauls another of the many special trains to be seen in the final years of steam operation. It is hauling the 'Dorset Coast Express' which travelled from Waterloo to Weymouth, with a special visit to the Swanage branch too. *John . H. Bird*

occurs on any train, which, thank goodness is very rare. On this occasion I kept a wary eye on it after Eastleigh, but my attention was drawn away from it by a passenger request for me to help in getting luggage ready for alighting at the next stop, which was by then Southampton. I did this job, and then went back to the front van only to find that the fire had restarted, and here we were in the middle of Southampton tunnel. My friend, Bill Churchill, from my Dorchester days, was now the Inspector at Southampton and he helped me put it out once more with the aid of a fire extinguisher issued for use on all electrical equipment. I didn't consider that the station would be in any danger from our arrival and to get some help would be the best under the circumstances. To prevent any further outbreak, I had the heating jumper from the engine to the train uncoupled. This meant that any air conditioning and heat to the buffet car would not be working, but we were only about 40 minutes away from our destination and I thought any discomfort, or lack of tea and coffee, was not worth taking any risk. Better safe than sorry. I now had with me one of the proper fire extinguishers that

Bill had given me just in case, which I had to return to him at the end of the journey.

Soon after that incident, I made up my mind that I would examine every fire extinguisher on every train that I worked. When in Clapham Junction yard on Sunday afternoon, ready to take out a train of nine empty coaches to Waterloo (before they took up a service from there to the West of England,) out of nine I took down from where they were strapped on at the ends of the carriages, seven were not working. My request for replacements was met with dismay by the foreman on duty, who said, 'You're bloody keen mate, aren't you?'. With much difficulty and I suspect, robbing of other trains, he produced five and promised that he would 'phone Waterloo to provide two more on arrival, which they did. Maybe it was coincidence, but soon after that each guard was required to attend fire courses at Eastleigh, fire precautions were drastically tightened up and never again did I find another extinguisher that didn't work. All trains were fitted with two types of fire extinguishers, which had to be regularly checked and signed on an attached form as being done.

When I first started as a guard there was insufficient time allowed for examination of a train, and to check inside and outside of it to my satisfaction. At first a lot of this was done in my own time, and there came a time when this was brought to the notice of management, who agreed that an examination should take place at Bournemouth West with local departmental committee and sectional council members present, along with local management and my Guards Inspector, who at this time was Bill Churchill. I had the honour of carrying out the examination, I tried not to try anything outside of what I normally did and the complete thing took 44 minutes, the time then allowed was under 20 minutes. Shortly after news came that we were to be allowed at least 30 minutes to examine any train and I felt proud to have been involved in securing that extra ten minutes.

For some unexplained reason it was decided that all guards at Bournemouth Central would be amalgamated with those at Bournemouth West carriage sidings, all of whom were passenger men, never ever working goods trains. This decision caused a few problems because it was not right that some of the older men at the West should now have to learn goods work at their age, and maybe some of the younger element would be demoted, as some of the men coming from the Central were senior in service.

The problems were sorted out by the formation of one link, the elders being catered for by making a link of six which would not roster goods work. At first this did not go down too well with the West men but it was the only real solution as I saw it. The one link was almost unheard of on the Southern region. What it meant, was that everybody did the same work, regardless of seniority. At it's inception there were only four elders at Bournemouth West who were considered too near retiring age to learn goods work and the

Two shots of a locomotive class that disappeared from BR in 1965. The Maunsell 'S15' class was a variant of the Urie class built in 1920. Nos. 30840 and 30823 are seen at speed in these evocative photographs.

This study by George Marsh of 'Merchant Navy' Class Pacific No. 35022 *Holland-Africa Line* shows a scene lost in Britain until the emergence of preserved locomotives on the main line again from the late 1970s.

link being for six members the other two were enlisted from those on light duties due to medical grounds, known as the 'green carders'. This sprang from any vehicle requiring attention for any minor defect and was allowed to travel, a green label was attached stating defect and place where repairs should be carried out after the end of it's current journey. As I had much to do with the instigation of it all I wasn't too popular at first, but it soon passed over, and in the end most said that it was for the better. If I say so myself, Bournemouth turned out to be one of the best depots on the Southern Region.

There is always somebody trying to upset the apple cart when all is going smoothly, and the upset came in the form of the four day week. nine hours forty five minutes a day with two days a week off, rest days. The management bods explained how nice it would be to have all that time off, especially the long weekends and painted a very rosy picture. In spite of protests from us older members it was introduced and we were into the '9 hours 45' era. Now I always reckoned that eight hours a day was long enough for anybody, by the time that you had to leave home and then get back again, or when the trains ran late, it was mostly at

least 10 or 11 hours away and having to get up around 4.a.m. that was enough for me. I didn't take to the additional hours roster. I knew when it started that it would not be possible to cover the whole of the rosters without having to work a rest day a week, sometimes two. There was sickness, annual leave and compensatory leave to be covered, and there were times when that could not be granted due to there being no cover. Whenever an application for any leave was refused it was the usual thing for the applicant to declare himself 'sick' and so to get his time off that way, and then a train or trains would have to be cancelled. Saturdays were the problem days for the roster clerks. Although very much in the minority there were guards at Bournemouth who would declare sick so as to miss the late turn. It was possible to look at a roster well in advance and predict that the man rostered for this or that shift on a Saturday evening turn would not be turning up. In any of the rosters there was always a man 'spare' who could cover any eventualities and if he wasn't used it was he who would have to do the shift.

After some time, management decided to send offenders up to the doctor at Southampton for a medical before confronting them with their record of sickness and for a while the 'spare' man could relax, but it didn't last long before it was back to normal. Sunday working was never included in the 39 hours working week and hours rostered on a Sunday was for anything between 7 and 10 hours. It worked out that you did every other Sunday although you might work two following and the next two off. An additional Sunday turn was a welcome bonus to a pay packet, but I crossed my name off the list because my weekends were looked forward to be off. If I worked it would only be on the early turn and I felt in fairness to my mates that I should not be allowed to pick and choose my turns. There were those who did, but I had my principles.

I had not had the good fortune to work steam hauled trains, when I came on as a guard. They were all electric or diesel and the main units in use on the main line were the R.E.P.S. These were made up of a four coach traction unit of 3200 horse power which would either haul or propel one or two T.C., units not powered but capable of being driven from. These were used on the fast and semi fast services from Bournemouth to Waterloo, and on arrival back in Bournemouth the T.C. units were detached and a diesel loco attached and ready to go forward to Weymouth, the electric rail only being installed as far as Branksome then. The usual teething problems were encountered with the R.E.P.S., mostly with the collecting shoes getting knocked off fairly frequently. I was surprised that this sort of thing could happen for the Southern had been running electric trains for over 60 years and didn't have this trouble on the Portsmouth and suburban lines. Modern technology and design fault I expect. However it was all overcome in the end and the R.E.P.S. gave good service. Stopping services were served by the V.E.P.S., another four car unit but of only about 1100 horse power each. Very reliable machines but every now and again the camshaft would cause problems and fail to run back and then it was a case of shutting the unit down completely for a few minutes, switching it back into circuit, and nine times out of ten it would be alright.

In the early 1950s the Southern Region built a number of two car units which were known as H.A.P.S. and were mostly used in suburban services to strengthen their overcrowded commuter trains. A few of these units found their way further south to us, and occasionally used on the Lymington branch, or on the 93 stopping services from Bournemouth to Waterloo. There was only one toilet, it was a non corridor; being older they were also a bit noisier than the modern stock, access to the drivers compartment was through the guards van, with a sliding door dividing them. Now and again a B.E.P. from the South Eastern division of the Southern Region, or a C.E.P. would appear on our lines. Before going further it would be as well to explain what all this R.E.P., V.E.P. etc., is all about, the E.P. stands for 'electric pneumatic' and denotes that the unit is fitted with a brake system of that name, the 'R' stands for restaurant which is included in the unit, the 'V' is for vestibule, the unit being made up of open coaches as opposed to closed compartments, with the exception of first class. The 'B' infers that there is a buffet in the unit, the 'C' means that it is a corridor train, mostly made up of closed compartments. These were my favourites, they were much in the style of the old Southern Railway coaches, they seemed to ride a little harder, fitted with 'Commonwealth' type bogies while most

of our stock had the new more modern 'type 2' bogies fitted.

Before it became all NetWork South East and all red, white and blue these South Eastern trains were a pleasant (to me anyway) 'Jaffa Cake' orange mixture. I never did take to our Union Jack shades, much preferred the Green of the old Southern. There was one good thing about the E.P.s. Providing that the unit, engine or vehicle was fitted it was possible to couple any type of unit and drive it from anywhere on a train so formed, even from something marshalled in the middle or even from the extreme rear. Every train was fitted with two types of brake; a Westinghouse air brake could be brought into use should the electric pneumatic brake fail, each brake was operated through a main reservoir tank situated under the guards compartment mainly, and charged up to between eighty five and a hundred and ten pounds pressure. Each application of the brake would use some of this air in the tank and the ticking noise that you could hear coming from under the train meant that the tank was being recharged, never dropping below the amount of air required to make either type of brake work at any time. Before any journey was commence it was a rule that the guard went to the rear drivers cab and after communicating with the driver, had a brake test of both systems to make sure that they were in working order.

A guards examination of electric trains were not so complex as on locomotive stock. I felt much more at home on them. The 'juicers' (as I called them) almost looked after themselves, but the loco hauled were something different again. Walking round each coach there were at least fifteen items to check on the outside and nearly as many on the inside, miss something and you were in for bother. Some of the sets that came to Bournemouth had seen better days. It was not unusual to encounter four different types of bogies on one train. In my early days as a guard it was possible for the train to be formed of coaches belonging to all four regions, sometimes including the Scottish region for good measure.

I call to mind one Saturday morning at Bournemouth West sidings having to wait for an engine to arrive before carrying out a brake test. After examination of my train, when it did finally arrive, I discovered that on the last bogie of the rear coach the brakes did not work. It is possible for a train to start without brakes working on a bogie or even perhaps two, providing that the coach is marshalled away from the rear of the train. A brake test is made by taking the pipe off the dummy on the last coach. If it is 'vacuum' braked, which this one was, it causes the brakes to be applied to the wheels, and you have to make sure that this is being done on the last three bogies of the train by pushing them with your foot and feeling no movement of the brake blocks. I have now to send for a fitter to attend to my last coach.

In the meantime I walked along the whole length of the train pushing on each brake block in turn and found five more bogies where the brakes were not working satisfactorily. We left for Poole to commence our journey with just one of the bogies brakes not working, permitted because it was in the middle of the train and ten coaches forming the train. After running round a Poole sidings I decided to have another quick look round and then found another coach with unsatisfactory brakes, this meant that while we could

The new era. A Class 33 diesel approaches Wareham level crossing with a train for Weymouth from Bournemouth. The route code is 91.

continue it would have to be at a reduced speed. On arrival at the platform I telephoned the Southern Control centre and told them of this, because any deviation of the line speed meant that the train might have to be held back somewhere en route to allow a faster one to precede. On arrival at Basingstoke I was told that the Eastern Region could not accept the train at reduced speed and that the second offending coach would have to be detached from the train before it reached Eastern Region metals, so off it had to come at Basingstoke.

One of the joys of a Winter morning is riding in a train behind an engine that cannot provide the necessary electrical train heat supply because it is not fitted to do so. There was only a few in service that had been converted to E.T.H. for working passenger trains, and the failure of one of these meant that a freight engine was pressed into service and the train was devoid of heating, air conditioning and lighting after the already low batteries gave out. No hot water or power to the microwave ovens in the buffet cars.

The appendix stated that a train could not commence a journey if it had no lights and every effort should be made to provide heating, a train to be on supply for at least half an hour from October to April on cold mornings. Despite protests from us guards these conditions existed for a long time. Complaints from long suffering passengers were all too frequent, apologies over the public address system were treated as a joke by our regulars. The usual excuse from the management was that a shortage of class 47 locomotives in the area accounted for trains having to be taken out in this condition.

I am aware that Joe Public is of the opinion that the majority of drivers and guards are a lot of 'bolshies', ready to down tools at the slightest sign of anything hierarchy comes up with, not so. To a man at Bournemouth the interests of our passengers have always been foremost, I always retained a very good relationship with our regulars and not so regulars. I can say that, so have the rest of my mates at the depot, but on one Thursday morning things came to a head on collision with authority that was much to the distaste of everyone of us.

On arriving at approximately nine o'clock this particular morning I was greeted by a good colleague of mine, Terry Snow, and told that he had been sent home by the train crew manager for refusing to take out a train with all the faults that I have mentioned. The usual practice was to sign on by telephone contacting the train crew supervisor at Bournemouth advising him of your presence and of the train that you were booked to take out. I did this and was told that the train crew manager would like a word with me. He came to the 'phone and informed me that I was now required to work the train that Terry had refused to take out. I had guessed that this might have happened so I told him that I was fully in agreement with the decision that my colleague had taken and therefore my attitude would be the same. This, of course, left him with no other course but to suspend me from duty also.

This happened to the next two men on duty, Mike Couchman and Fred Chaffey, after being advised what had gone on before their arrival they also refused duty. The four of us then decided that enough was enough, the present atmosphere that we were working under could not continue, and so we contacted each guard who had signed on that morning and told them of what had happened, and to a man, within an hour a withdrawal of labour was agreed upon.

We were told that the guilty four would be issued with a Form 1 (charge sheet) and were booked to appear before the Area Manager, Mr Hacker, the next morning. Rightly or Wrongly I always felt that the inexperience of our managers were more than half responsible for the conditions that we had to put up with. Both the Train Crew Manager and the Area Manager were young men of very limited railway workings, their reasoning being that it was better to run a cold and dark train than no train at all, and if you were not prepared to do that then you had better consider your occupation as being elsewhere.

You could say that this was good reasoning perhaps, but it had been going on for a long time and looked set to continue for the duration of the winter. Somebody had to make a stand on behalf of our fare paying passengers, heaven knows, the fares are high enough without having to sit in freezing conditions with the doors on the ends of the coaches propped open with the passengers luggage if need be, to allow for the absence of the air conditioning; no teas or coffees, or if there was, only until the canister of hot water ran out that was provided at the starting point.

The only hardship we caused was to the aged and infirm passengers who found that crossing London was an extreme or impossible handicap. It was still possible for passengers to travel via the capital city and change there for all the destinations that our cross country trains served, as Bournemouth was the only depot on strike and trains were still running crewed by other depots.

I was very sad to have got involved in a thing of this nature, especially after I could count on the fingers of one hand the number of times that I had supported a strike, and I never ever worked during one, in nearly fifty years of service.

A meeting with the Union Representative was arranged for the next day, friday. He had somehow arranged for the Form 1s to be withdrawn and after a somewhat stormy meeting it was agreed that the whole thing was unofficial and to put our case on a firmer standing it would be as well for us to return to work, which we did the next morning, saturday. No publicity can be likened to bad publicity and a few days later in the letter column of the local press there was a letter printed from two nurses who were very much inconvenienced by our action and very critical of the guards at Bournemouth. It was obvious that I could not let that go undefended and I wrote to that same paper offering our sincere apologies and stating our case, and the cause of the dispute, and hoping that if ever it was the misfortune of anyone of us to require treatment at that particular hospital, they might understand that it was not our aim to inconvenience anyone but to ensure that future journeys might be on a nice, warm and well lit train. Bless their hearts, they wrote back and said sorry but they hadn't understood at the time what it was all about. A footnote to this episode, when I came on duty on the Saturday morning early turn, there was not one but two E.T.H. fitted 47 class locomotives in the depot!!

Things improved for a little while but as always

standards were set to fall. As time went on so did the reliability of our stock and locomotives, maintenance dates were not observed, about the only things available at Bournemouth West for 47s were fuel, oil and water. The 33 class locos didn't fair much better and it wasn't uncommon for at least two a day to fail somewhere between Bournemouth and Weymouth. Connections were not held at Bournemouth and passengers for a fast service to London living anywhere west of Bournemouth took a gamble and very often had to settle for a semi-fast service arriving a lot later in London. Electrification of the line from Branksome to Weymouth proved a godsend to these people and a much better service and a more reliable one.

Many more problems were to follow with the introduction of new trains to the area, namely the 442s, with the new seating style, aircraft type seats. They were not popular with our commuters who promptly christened them 'Plastic Pigs'. I know of many of our regulars at Winchester who would wait for one of the conventional trains as they put it, rather than catch a plastic one. After the now well worn Reps they seemed to me to be a lot smoother running, but in units of five cars were not the answer to ideal commuter trains as only two units could be coupled together on any one service due to the length of platforms on our stations. This of course shortened trains by two coaches although it was argued that there were more seats available.

There were many problems experienced with the operation of the 'pug' doors. It had been known for them to open while the train was in motion. I know this to be true, it happened on one of mine. Opening and closing the doors was the responsibility of the guard, the switches for this being in a box in the corridor opposite to the compartment door and brought into use by a key inserted in a lock on the panel. A button had to be pressed by a passenger when it was lit up to open or close the doors; two separate buttons provided for such an operation if the guard was stranded in the train whilst carrying out his duties examining tickets and arriving at a station. Then he would have to wend his way back through the masses to his van to let everybody on and off. A couple of times I jumped out of my van at a station, completely forgetting to operate my switches and the porter enquiring of me if it was my intention to let anyone get out today.

Before the 442s came into general service I was rostered to be the guard on one from Bournemouth to Weymouth and back to Bournemouth Carriage sidings with members of the Railway Inspectorate, representatives from the Derby builders, and other high ranking railway officials, all wanting to see how the unit would perform; and what a let down it turned out to be. I was asked by a member of the Inspectorate to demonstrate just what would happen on a normal journey when the doors would be required to be opened, the doors on the front three coaches could be opened while the rear two coaches remained closed, or doors on the whole five coaches could all be opened at the same time, depending on the length of the platform. The first stop at Poole was on the Up platform, the line being reversible to allow another train on the down line to precede if need be. Nothing went right; some doors could be opened, some not, this went on all down the line to Weymouth. On departure from there a start was made from the platform with the doors open but within seconds had closed, success at last. Then it was decided, after the driver had been informed, to see if the train would stop if the door was made to open whilst the train was in motion. This was attempted after leaving Bincombe tunnel, and again was a success, much to the relief of the Derby reps., on board. I thought at the time that so much still had to be done before the units were accepted by Network South East and to the satisfaction of the Ministry of Transport people that a decision of 'not yet' would be a foregone conclusion, but I was wrong...... At a meeting held on the train for a couple of hours after lunch, they were won over by the Derby people who said that an alteration here and a modification there and it would work out alright.

When the units finally came into service, these same Derby people were riding on some units seeing to faults as they occurred. The doors were always a problem, when the train came to a stand where the platform was on a curve and the line was leaning, Clapham Junction, Beaulieu Road and Christchurch are stations that spring to mind. Then the doors had to be assisted to close, the motor not being strong enough to cope with the additional weight imposed on it, another modification. The three door and two door openings were abandoned, and all five coaches doors were made to open. On a ten coach semi-fast train this meant that only the front trains doors would opened where there was short platforms, and many passengers were carried on past their destinations who were riding in the rear parts of the train, especially the young mums with their babes and pushchairs, and the old folks with their suitcases trying to get up the train before it restarted.

I think it was around 1971 when it was decided that the main function of guards would be to check and issue tickets and to be a general mobile booking clerk and ticket inspector. This enabled many stations to become just 'halts', with no staff in attendance and what was now to be known as 'open stations'. Many of my colleagues had no previous experience of ever issuing tickets or dealing with fraudsters whose sole intention was to ride in a train without paying the fare. I was perhaps lucky in that in my early days at Hamworthy Junction I had been taught office work and experienced a few of it's mysteries. A day with an Inspector who explained how to work out fares and write out tickets and you were on your own. Masses of books with fares and instructions were issued. An excess fare pad and two pounds in change, one was now qualified to issue tickets to anywhere in the United Kingdom. This was great when it came to local fares but even they sometimes were a bit of a problem when it came to availability of tickets on trains before a certain time; frequent

alterations were made; some tickets done away with, such as the 'weekend' ones. There were things that you could not get into your brainbox due to there being so many. In a crowded train such as the 18.30 from Waterloo on a Friday night some fares had to be made up from out of your head, tickets issued illegally. You were supposed to ask for the full fare and not accept discount railcards where the passenger boarded the train where the booking office was open and he could have bought a ticket. Try telling that to a passenger arriving at Waterloo to find a queue a mile long and the train due to depart in the next five minutes; use your discretion was the advice given to me and so I did. I used to say to them (my passengers) that perhaps the booking clerk had closed the office for calls of nature, they would agree and I would have to believe them. It was not uncommon to have collected up to ú300 on arrival at Bournemouth and still not having checked the front one or two coaches by then.

The author at Bournemouth West in Intercity days, 1993.

A new grade of assistant train ticket examiners were introduced but their duties only took them as far at first, Bournemouth to Southampton, mostly on stopping services which was alright but they were sorely needed on the busier services at weekends and were never available. You might occasionally have a ticket inspector from Waterloo down to Winchester with you which made the job much easier but it didn't happen very often.

All this heralded the introduction of the 'Driver only' operated trains, no guard required. This was the norm in the London area but not so much down here at the present, but have no fear, it will come and in the not too distant future either. How the driver will be able to cope in any emergency remains to be seen. Teaching an old dog new tricks is a hard job at the best of times but trying to make an old guard into a brand new booking clerk, come everything else, was nigh impossible, until the younger men came along who, during their training, the art became part of the curriculum. Customer care one day courses were introduced to bring in the new grade of 'Conductor Guard'. We were shown how to treat our customers,as passengers were now to be called; how to cope in times of delays, and to keep everyone informed whenever anything went wrong. Now I thought that we always did that, not always well, but sometimes information was not always forthcoming and then it became a hard job to placate irate passengers incensed by the continuing delay and not knowing why. Little white lies sometimes came into it to try and ease the situation, but it was mainly the truth that I stuck to and was occasionally unkind in my comments when I thought that delay could or should have been avoided. Engineering works at weekends were another bone of contention, lines being closed from Saturday to Monday mornings necessitating diversions and or bus services replacing the train. Once again inconveniencing our passengers and adding much time to their journeys which,if they had travelled from the Midlands or North, they had no knowledge of the additional time that it would take to get to where they were going. Again try to explain to a dear old lady who was being met by some relation that she should have been told that there was engineering works on the line before she set out. It was highly probable that the authorities there didn't know either. The guard is always the fall guy, next man to take the can for everything that happens on, and to his train. Points failures, track circuit failures, loss of traction current, failure of trains in front, lineside fires, they all add up to the guard requiring the wisdom of Solomon and the patience of Job

I didn't like sitting in a train that was stopped and not to be told why, and I knew my passengers didn't either, and so I did my best to find out the cause of any hold up and then try to guess how long the delay would last, (I was gifted with the luck of the devil and was never very far out), not always possible on a long train with the P.A. system not available or not working. Then it meant going through each coach repeating what you had to say at least twice, and then trying to answer all the queries that followed, and then a complaint from a passenger because they had not been told the reason for the hold up.

I never did carry any form of alcoholic drink when I was working but a colleague at Waterloo had insisted on my accepting an amount of Brandy that had been given to him as a present and so I put it away in my guards bag and almost forgot it was there, not particularly fond of brandy anyway. In later weeks this action was to nearly backfired on me. We were passing a bridge on the London side of Farnborough where vandals threw a stone through the window of a carriage where an old lady was seated with her daughter and a young lady with a very young baby. They were not hurt but both the old lady and the young lady suffered shock, the stone just missing her baby. I managed to comfort her first and move them to another seat away from the broken glass and then went to see the elderly lady who seemed not to be too well. Her daughter told me that she had previously suffered heart problems and it was then that I remembered the half bottle of brandy. I went back to my van and brought it to her and suggested that the lady might benefit by a small amount to steady her heart beat rate. After departure from Woking I went back to where they were now seated to find that it had had the desired effect and that the lady was now much better. I had also offered the young mother some brandy which she declined but at Woking I had arranged for her to be met at Waterloo where someone would help her and the babe to a taxi before continuing on her journey.

The outcome of all this was that they both wrote a letter of appreciation to the authorities at Waterloo saying what a kind and helpful guard I had been, even down to supplying a bottle of brandy to aid recovery. I received a copy of this letter with the thanks of the management endorsed and no mention of the brandy of which I should not have been in possession whilst on duty. This stone throwing is quite a problem on the railways, especially during the school holidays, and on 'known' estates where

troublemakers are apt to amuse themselves by indulging in the dangerous practice. In my own area I would rate my old station at Hamworthy Junction as a hazard spot and not well liked by our train crews at Bournemouth.

This was where again one day one of my trains became a victim of some of these louts and a brick was thrown through the window narrowly missing two young lads and their parents, landing on the seat opposite to where they were sitting, and broken glass all over the seat and floor, which meant that the whole train had to come out of service on arrival at Bournemouth.

I have mentioned that a good many of us were not equipped to deal with people committing a fraud on the railway. I was one of them I freely admit. I could never work out if the person was genuine or not. It was my experience that the little old lady sat in the corner would burst into tears at the slightest suggestion that she was travelling illegally with either a ticket out of date or indeed, no ticket at all, was the biggest and most frequent twister of all. The barrister attending court at Winchester was not past trying to get away without paying; and I once heard a good story from any army officer in charge of a unit on the Salisbury Plain when he was unable to produce a ticket on a train; and so you will understand when I say that I considered everyone guilty until they could prove otherwise and there are a few that did not travel past the next station when I was guard on the service.

The regular commuters were great people to deal with, the higher their station in life the better and more understanding of any situation they were. What I would call the 'bumped up' middle class were always out to be awkward and sometimes downright rude, not all of them thank goodness, but you soon got to know who to pass the time of day with and who not to. If I had a favourite train in those days it would have been the 6.18 a.m. from Bournemouth to Waterloo and the 18.45 Waterloo to Bournemouth back. The up 6.18 a.m. was the one involved in the Clapham Junction disaster in which I lost many friends among those killed, including John Rolls and Arthur Creech the two drivers. A very sad day for everyone, but none more than for all of us at Bournemouth train crews depot.

The frailties of human nature often shows its ugly side among passengers on trains, thank goodness in the minority of them, but no less unpleasant when encountered. 'I will sit where I want to sit', (even though there is a reserved label attached), 'I will put my cases where I will', (even in the gangway), are among many things that have to be attended to. 'No Smoking' signs are not to be heeded by some; tell a person to either turn down a noisy radio or turn it off altogether and you are met with a load of abuse, 'show me where I can't have it on' is the usual response.

I recall the day when a passenger came to my van to complain that a lady was occupying the seat that was reserved for him. This meant that I had to come and ask this particular lady to move, but on arriving at the seat found that there was no label to say that it was reserved. The train already being well patronised, I then had to place this gentleman in a first class seat, one of a few that was not already reserved as well, probably depriving a first class passenger of a seat further along the line. On going through the train examining tickets a little later a passenger informed me that the good lady sat opposite (who was the person involved earlier) had on taking the seat removed the reservation label and put it in her handbag. Oh! that he had told me that at the time, but she had got out at the previous station and I could do nothing.

It always amazed me that people could take away even the kitchen sink when travelling on trains and then moan like the devil about having no one to give them help when they got off. A young mother with a small babe in a pushchair and three or four cases, on her own was an everyday occurrence; young children sent hundreds of miles on their own with a request for the guard to keep an eye on him or her, 'there will be somebody to meet them at the other end', was the normal information passed on. It is virtually impossible to be responsible for the well being of children on journeys. You can't be there all the time, and I always informed parents, or other people sending children on their own that I was not prepared to accept the responsibility for what they should be doing.

Thieves were another modern day problem, I say the word 'modern', thieving today is down to a fine art as the saying goes. Young and old are skilled in depriving passengers of cameras, purses and other items left on the seats while the unwary one goes to the toilet or for a cup of tea. Suitcases left in the luggage space at the end of the coach disappear whenever the train arrives at any station; anything left in the toilet, even for a few seconds, are never handed to the guard. I was a victim myself of this on two occasions, once when I took off my watch and forgot it was there, went back within a minute or so and it was gone, enquiries among my passengers failed to find it. The second time I was on a late running commuter train having hurriedly transferred from a failed unit to another train and I put my blue cash bag in my trouser pocket with many other things. In my rush and on boarding the replacement train it dropped down on to the floor just outside my van; after putting down everything else I went to pick it up, and as with my watch it had disappeared.

I had faintly observed an elderly man pass by who stooped down as he went, but a thorough search of the train and again enquiring of my passengers failed to find any trace of the bag and sixteen pounds in small change which was in it. It is a sign of the times that we live in, unfortunately, if we all took the precautions that were needed to safeguard our property at any time then we would all own a huge safe that when opened by any thief would emit a highly poisonous gas that would shrivel their thieving hands down to a stump, but even then I suspect that they would find a way of working with their feet.

I have mentioned children travelling on their own. Another such 'hazard' that we have had to deal with is the person that is put on the train and is subject to many forms of 'fits', or has just had a heart attack, or is heavily pregnant when you are expected to be trained to deal with any emergencies that may arise en route. Drug takers are among the worst, you cannot always recognise the symptoms, but always have to try and do something about the violence that goes with this particular evil. One morning just after leaving Basingstoke on a Waterloo bound semi-fast train from Bournemouth the lady stewardess came to see me and said

that a man had attacked, among others, a lady and her daughter in the restaurant car, and would I come and sort it out. Well, it is no good thinking about what you might have to do, you just have to leave what you are doing and go. When I arrived on the scene I was told by a man standing at the bar where I could find the culprit, and he came with me to point out a man stood with two others in the gangway between the first and second coach of the train. He seemed to be in normal conversation with the two men stood with him when the door opened and a little old gentleman came forward, only to be immediately set upon by one of the men. There was nothing I could do other then try to restrain him and this I did by pulling on his long hair, causing him to fall to the ground. I shouted to the old gentleman to get back to his seat as quick as he could, and with the aid of the other two passengers managed to walk the crazed man back to the caged part of the guards van, and after locking the two external doors I fetched a chair from the restaurant car and made him sit down, and locked the cage doors making him look like a trapped animal. I then had to take statements from passengers who had been his victims. The little old gentleman had come to see if it was now alright for his wife to proceed to the toilet as the first time that she had tried she was prevented from doing so, being attacked by the man in my cage. On arrival at Woking I sought the assistance of the station supervisor to get the police to arrest him and get him off my train. The supervisor was a young, well built man who asked me to take him to where this character was, which I did.

I unlocked the doors and my colleague made an attempt to reason with him but was met with a storm of abuse and a young porter got a small radio full in his face while stood at the door. My mate then got hold of him and threw him on to the platform, 'right Michael, on your way, I'll see to him' he said and we were on our way once more. In the meantime I had picked up a letter while clearing up the mess in the van and on arrival at Waterloo I 'phoned Woking and gave the supervisor a name and address on the envelope, 'yes, that's him' he said, 'it took three policemen to take him away in the end'. The name and address was that of a doctor living in Southampton, though if he was a doctor of medicine I never found out.

Still on the subject of doctors; there was an elderly retired surgeon that would always travel on the 1.00 p.m. from Bournemouth, boarding the train at Christchurch, alighting at Southampton, then going on to Romsey to visit an old friend. It was always his pleasure to sit in the guards seat during his journey and talk of not much other than trains, being a keen railway buff he knew more about the railways than I did. I enjoyed his conversations, but we crossed swords one day when the subject of drug abusers came up and he said that he felt sorry for those that were so afflicted. 'I can't see how you can say that' I told him, 'the majority of them knew what they were letting themselves in for when they started on drugs' but no amount of reasoning by me would change his mind. But never again did we ever get involved on that subject, for all that I was very fond of the old gentleman and looked forward to his company even though I had to stand from Christchurch to Southampton each time.

The behaviour of young lads travelling short distances on local trains needed some watching. School holidays are the worst time for mischief seeking boys (and sometimes girls). I have caught these youngsters setting fire to paper in the toilets, throwing light bulbs and seating out of the window, tampering with parcels and mails in the front van of the train, getting into the guards van compartment in his absence and turning off the lights and generally creating chaos and then have it happen again, openly defying any form of authority, and wondering if their parents had any idea as to where they were or even if they cared. But just strike one in anger and the law is down on you like a ton of bricks for assault.

The final chapter.